Change Your Bad Habits for Good!

Change Your Bad Habits for Good!

Audrey Beslow

Abingdon Press
Nashville

CHANGE YOUR BAD HABITS FOR GOOD!

Copyright © 1989 by Abingdon Press

All rights reserved.
No part of this work may be reproduced or transmitted in any form or by any means, electronic or mechanical, including photocopying and recording, or by any information storage or retrieval system, except as may be expressly permitted by the 1976 Copyright Act or in writing from the publisher. Requests for permission should be addressed in writing to Abingdon Press, 201 Eighth Avenue South, Nashville, TN 37202.

This book is printed on acid-free paper.

BESLOW, AUDREY, 1931-
　Change your bad habits for good! / Audrey Beslow.
　　p.　cm.
　ISBN 0-687-06044-3 (alk. paper)
　1. Habit breaking—Religious aspects—Christianity. I. Title.
BV4598.7.B47　　1989
241'.4—dc19　　　　　　　　　　　　　　　　　　　88-26842
　　　　　　　　　　　　　　　　　　　　　　　　　　　CIP

Scripture quotations unless otherwise marked are from the Revised Standard Version of the Bible, copyright 1946, 1952, 1971 by the Division of Christian Education of the National Council of Churches of Christ in the USA. Used by permission.

Scripture quotations marked NIV are taken from the *Holy Bible: New International Version.* Copyright © 1973, 1978, 1984 by the International Bible Society. Used by permission of Zondervan Bible Publishers.

MANUFACTURED BY THE PARTHENON PRESS AT
NASHVILLE, TENNESSEE, UNITED STATES OF AMERICA

*This book is dedicated to
Richard John Sullivan,
my good friend of many years,
whose adventurous spirit, warm laugh, and
caring presence enriched the
lives of many people.*

*Called to appear before the throne
of God and begin new adventures February 21, 1988.*

CONTENTS

Foreword by Ralph Osborne   9

Introduction   11

PART ONE : *Reviewing Old Habits*   13
1. How Habits Control Our Lives   15
2. Habits Resulting from Fear   30

PART TWO : *Establishing New Habits*   43
3. Motivation:
Tool #1 for Building a Habit   45
4. Knowledge:
Tool #2 for Building a Habit   60
5. Practice:
Tool #3 for Building a Habit   73

PART THREE : *Choosing Habits for a Lifetime*   91
6. Relating Our Habits to God   93
7. Habits of Thinking   116
8. Habits of Relationship   135
9. Balancing Habits   151

Conclusion   159

FOREWORD

READING THIS BOOK HAS PUT ME IN TOUCH with a whole range of behavior patterns that I hadn't ever bothered to examine. I didn't even realize they were there! Thanks to Audrey Beslow, I am beginning to rethink and restate my long-term and short-term goals and then to check out my habit patterns to see whether they are helping me toward those goals or acting as a hindrance. She has also helped me recognize how much I resist this process of reevaluation: "Laziness and narcissism seem to dominate the workings of the human body and mind"!

Be warned in advance—that is what this book will do for (and to!) the reader. Audrey Beslow provides us with very helpful insights into what habits are and how and why we give them dominant places in our lives. Then she provides us excellent tools whereby we can develop habits that will be helpful to us for a lifetime. Questions and exercises help us apply the material she has so clearly presented.

Audrey Beslow's clear orientation is that of a thinking, believing, practicing Christian. It will not come as a surprise, therefore, to arrive at chapter 6 and find a very helpful section entitled "Relating Our Habits to God." There she helps us think through our "life goals." In her words, "a life goal needs to be an interest that continues until death and is never finished, but has triumphs along the way."

Pushing us yet further, the writer urges us to consider two areas that often are neglected in presentations on habits: our habits of thinking and our habits of relationship. Again, questions and exercises walk us through the processes of self-examination, determining available choices, and selected new or better ways of doing things, which can be developed into positive, time-freeing, energy-saving habits.

By the time the reader has worked through the forty-six exercises in this book, insights will have been gained, challenges will have been confronted, choices will need to be made, and a new and more intentional set of habits will be available to make life work better and smoother.

With all of this, I need to say that I have watched Audrey Beslow not only do what she has written about here but also assist young people in her classes and adults in her seminars and workshops to a better way of thinking, responding, and behaving. It works! I've seen it! It will work for you as well!

Ralph Osborne
First Presbyterian Church of Hollywood
Hollywood, California

INTRODUCTION

A FEW YEARS AGO, MY PASTOR ASKED ME TO teach a class on discipline in our church's lay academy. I laughed, since I thought of myself as one needing more self-discipline, not as one who could teach it. But since they were planning way ahead and I had nearly a year to whip myself into shape, I thought, "Why not?" Although I didn't manage to become the disciplined person I had hoped, I did develop some new habits and recognized that I can continue to form and change habits the rest of my life. I realized that adults do not need to remain victims of their pasts but can make changes, one habit at a time.

God has created all human beings with the ability to gradually change their bodies, minds, and personalities into more and more powerful instruments to serve God and to fulfill their goals. The purpose of this book is to enable Christians

Keeping a Journal

to use the way God created us as habitual creatures to become more able servants of Jesus Christ.

If you are serious about changing your habit structure, then you will find it valuable to keep a notebook to record your responses to the exercises you choose to do. Although you could read this book in an evening, developing habits that will enable you to maximize your potential will take years. Actually, we are never finished changing habits since we are continually growing and seeing new dimensions to pursue.

Therefore, a record of the thoughts you have in reading each chapter will help you wisely select habits to work on now and in coming months. To add one habit per month is a fast pace; so you need a way to remember and a place to make plans.

PART ONE

Reviewing Old Habits

1

How Habits Control Our Lives

WHAT ARE HABITS? HABITS ARE LEARNED responses to stimuli. When we consistently respond to a cue in the same way without thinking, we have a habit. We have physical habits, such as the automatic hand lift to the doorknob. We have mental habits, such as regularly thinking of certain people or subjects. We have emotional and attitudinal habits, including worry, nagging, courtesy, or optimism, along with specific triggers for emotions that we each have developed over the years.

We all have hundreds of habits that we have never examined. Since our habits of action, thought, and attitude determine every decision we make and the person we will be the rest of our lives, it is essential that we review and revise these patterns periodically. We are products of our habits, not of our intentions.

Habits are the patterns we have formed in our attempts to fill our basic needs. William Glasser tells us in *Reality Therapy* (New York: Harper & Row, 1965) that although we all have basic needs (to love and be loved, to feel worth, etc.), we have established different patterns in our attempts to fulfill these needs. We continue with the same habits of behavior even if our methods are irresponsible or self-defeating because we assume this conduct is getting us what we need. We are often completely ignorant of our own damaging habit patterns unless we can get someone else's objective view.

The Control Panel and the Comfort Zone

Almost everything we do is a habit. William James says, "Habit is thus a second nature . . . as regards its importance in adult life; for the acquired habits of our training have by that time inhibited or strangled most of the natural impulsive tendencies which were originally there. Ninety-nine hundredths or, possibly, nine hundred ninety-nine thousandths of our activity is purely automatic and habitual, from our rising in the morning to our lying down each night" (*Talks to Teachers on Psychology* [New York: W. W. Norton, 1958], p. 57).

Since any action that had no negative feedback from it is likely to be repeated, we have habits of varying intensities. Some are thread-like habits—simply an inclination in a direction.

Routines that have been with us for years will continue without thought but can be altered without too much trauma. For a person who learned to drive in a stick-shift car, relearning the clutch habit is simple, even after many years of driving an automatic transmission. After only a few stops, the left foot works automatically. It may even wave around for a few days, back in the automatic car. Some habits can be pulled out of storage when needed and be put away again quite easily. But habits that satisfy an emotional need change only with great effort.

If we think of our minds as having a conscious or aware part and a subconscious or not-as-accessible part, this latter part is responsible for self-image. The subconscious attempts to preserve the psychological self—the deepest image of self, whatever the subconscious determines the "self" to be.

Our self-image—the truth and lies we believe about ourselves, the negative or positive effect each thought and experience has had on us, and our deepest desires and dreams—is what we are comfortable with because it is familiar; it is known. Therefore, this is our comfort zone, even if we don't like what we are. All habits become part of that comfort zone, because habits are comfortable. To create a new habit or get rid of an old habit necessitates changing our comfort zones, which function as our control panels, dictating how we respond to input from the world.

Figure 1
CONTROL PANEL

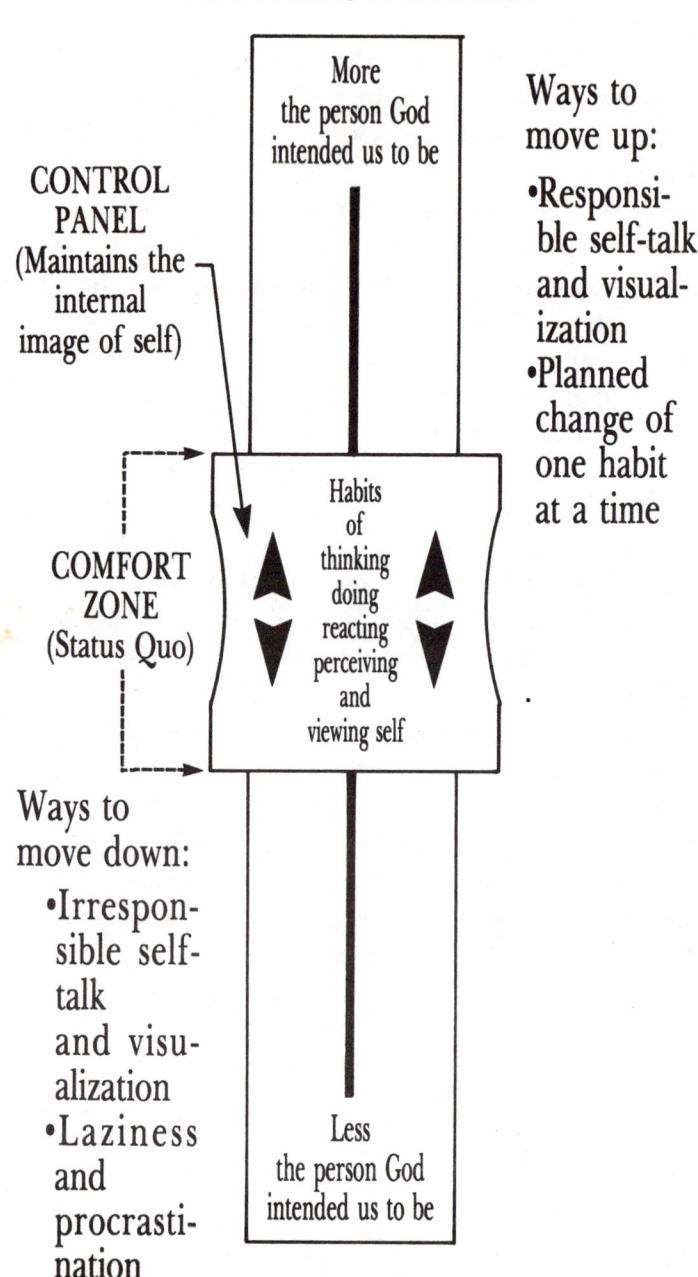

More
the person God
intended us to be

CONTROL PANEL
(Maintains the internal image of self)

Habits of thinking doing reacting perceiving and viewing self

COMFORT ZONE
(Status Quo)

Ways to move up:
- Responsible self-talk and visualization
- Planned change of one habit at a time

Ways to move down:
- Irresponsible self-talk and visualization
- Laziness and procrastination

Less
the person God
intended us to be

How Habits Control Our Lives

As we can see, habits pervade our whole lives, both the conscious and unconscious portions, but precisely since they are *learned* responses, they can be unlearned. The fact that habits are learned gives humans the choice to control their own lives. And choice to change makes us responsible for our habits, because laziness, following the path of least resistance, or remaining in our comfort zones are also choices.

The Results of Our Habits

When we observe an eighty-year-old, we see the results of eight decades of thoughts and attitudes: the sweetness or bitterness, the fear or trust, the wisdom or foolishness, the total self-centeredness or the interest in others, God, and knowledge. A lifetime of thinking and feeling has etched grooves that remain; thoughts that were hidden now become spoken. Even if memory grows fuzzy, old habit patterns of reacting and thinking remain.

Our eating habits obviously affect our shapes; less obviously they affect our health. Our exercise habits produce results we can see and feel in a few months, or even more obviously in a few years.

The effects of our social habits may be more difficult to discern, but they are as surely there: courteous words point us in a more caring direction; angry responses tend to make us increasingly abrasive; secret cheating or honesty today sets a pattern for tomorrow.

Our habits of thinking limit our perspectives to a worm's eye view or expand them to take in the universe. Our attitudes open us to joy or bind us to misery. Our habits of aligning our thoughts with truth keep us in touch with reality. Our habits of ignoring truths lead us toward whatever lies and evil persist in our environment. Our spiritual habits lead us toward God or away from the Creator.

Automatic routines can accomplish all the basic repetitive actions and thoughts of our lives and free our minds for creative work, if we deliberately program them effectively. Consider how good it would feel to have more time to pursue your interests. What if all the regular duties of life were so automatic that your energy, mind, and the bulk of your time could be focused on loving the people around you, pursuing creative activities, and enjoying life and God? What if interruptions were no problem because you had developed the habit of flexibility? What if anxiety never bothered you because you had dealt with the habits of fear and the negative thought patterns that cause anxiety?

On the other hand, consider how much the habit of laziness keeps us from being successful. We don't take the time to decide what habits would be valuable, or we waste time fighting ourselves, trying to keep the decisions we have already made. Or we procrastinate until tomorrow, after Christmastime, when the kids leave, when we retire. But tomorrow never comes.

Many of our habits are in conflict with our stated goals and cause us confusion and contradiction. We may say that our goal is to love God, but we habitually worry about money. We may say that we desire to love our neighbor as ourselves, but our habitual routine does not allow time for our neighbor. We may say that we love truth, but we routinely reiterate what we hear or half remember without checking its accuracy. We are the product of our habits, not of our intentions.

Laziness Determines Our Habits

All too often, laziness and narcissism seem to dominate the workings of the human body and mind. Unless some motivation and effort intervene, we human beings tend to put forth the least amount of energy possible to meet our perceived needs.

Inertia represents the same phenomenon in the physical world. Physical objects tend to stay as they are, at rest or in motion. Our bodies generally return to a stable condition after a disruption. In a similar way, the mind clings to the habits that have already been built to protect the inner self.

The American desire for a quick fix exemplifies both laziness and narcissism. We don't want to take the time and energy to develop healthy eating habits (laziness) so we go on a crash diet to look attractive for a coming function (narcissism). Our credit cards also give evidence to the habit of the quick fix.

It is easier to fall into habits of vice or inertia than habits of kindness and growth, because of our natural inclination toward self-centeredness and laziness. Any time we follow the path of least resistance, we are probably developing habits to serve these natural non-growth tendencies.

The lazy person doesn't invest the energy necessary to investigate which habits may be damaging. It takes effort to evaluate habits of thinking learned in childhood. But some of these patterns were based on false information. If money was a constant theme of conversation in a home, and winning the lottery was the family's highest concept of success, the children may have grown up with a view of money as omnipotent and themselves as victims. They may lack knowledge of how to be responsible for their own success and remain dependent on the whim of luck or the fantasy of the jackpot.

Laziness keeps us from the work of loving—doing that which is for the spiritual growth of another—and laziness keeps us from disciplining ourselves, because effort is required to achieve self-discipline. When we are prompted to phone a friend in need or to send a card to someone sick, and postpone the act until it is too late, that is laziness. When we plan to get some exercise but watch the news through three times instead, that is laziness. When we buy one more unnecessary outfit for ourselves but haven't money to give to the poor, that is narcissism. Unless we continue to develop habits of discipline to overcome our natural laziness, we will limit our growth and achievement.

Laziness can even keep us from communicating with God, since it is easier to complain or talk without listening than to struggle to understand. Communication implies a two-way communication, which takes patience and time, especially when we are talking with God.

The Principle of Inertia

Maintaining the status quo is a deeply ingrained habit of keeping everything the same and fearing change. The principle of inertia (maintaining the status quo), which is ingrained in the physical universe, is also ingrained in human behavior.

The inertia principle works like the cruise control of a car. It automatically brings behavior back to the established comfort zone. People who perceive themselves as B students will, if they receive a C, automatically put forth extra effort to get back into the B category. However, an A is also outside the comfort zone and will allow a little sloughing off until the grades are back to "normal." Habitual B students are more likely to perceive an A as an accident or the result of an easy teacher than as a reflection of their ability.

To change the setting of the comfort zone, or that which seems "normal," requires a change of perception that may be achieved through accurate knowledge and reinforced through self-talk, which will be discussed in chapter 4.

Exercise 1: Lazy Habits

1. What habits of laziness do you want to change or eliminate?

Our Self-image and Our Past

Not only are our actions affected by habit, but so are our thoughts. John Dewey tells us, "The medium of habit filters all the material that reaches our perception and thought" (*Human Nature and Conduct* [New York: Modern Library, 1958], p. 32).

Our self-images were originally formed by all the impressions that came into our minds and our own peculiar interpretation of those impressions as they related to ourselves. Because individuals have different processes of interpretation, two people will have different interpretations of the same impression.

Every stimulus that we receive is automatically filtered by our past experience, as we look for an association that can place this perception within an existing framework. The new experience or information not only fits into a knowledge schema, but takes on the emotional tone of that association and will be evaluated accordingly as good or bad, dangerous or safe, desirable or undesirable, true or false, negative or positive, boring or interesting, helpful or damaging, sense or nonsense. The response is almost instantaneous, bypassing our conscious thought processes.

For example, a single word can create an emotional response that affects every word that follows, or everything associated with the person who used the word. Hearing the word "book" might trigger boredom, avoidance, and fear, or pleasure, safety, and success. Each unchallenged evaluation reinforces the image that is already in place. For the book-hater, the image of avoiding activities related to books and people who speak of them may become so ingrained that a generalized sense of failure may pervade him when he is in any contact with a book-oriented world. Or, he may automatically dislike anyone who talks about books.

Certain tones of voice can trigger emotional reactions that originate so far back we can't identify the source. Gestures, atmospheres, colors, facial expressions, and appearance as well as many other items or impressions can all affect our emotional evaluation of the input we receive. These pre-judgments affect our reaction to the world around us and therefore our feelings about how well we fit into the world, how accepted we are, how capable we are, and how safe we are. These are all automatic responses to cues. They too are habits, and they affect everything we do.

Imagine that a young pastor sees a large, florid woman advancing toward him with a wide smile, holding out a gift-wrapped box. He immediately backs off, looks stern, and puts his hands behind his back. The woman looks crushed until someone pokes the young man and says, "That's for you, Jack," and Jack covers his faux pas with a laugh. Examining his reaction later, he recalls that the woman reminded him of an overbearing aunt who always gave him scratchy underwear for Christmas and expected a big kiss when he opened his package. He had hated the cornered feeling and had responded to the current gift-bearer with the same rebellion he had felt as a child.

Since the goal of the subconscious (in addition to preserving life) is to fulfill the deepest images the mind holds, in a conflict between the conscious and the subconscious, the subconscious wins. If my conscious mind says that I have good information to add to a political discussion and I should speak up, but my comfort zone says that political discussions are not safe, I will feel great stress if I speak because I am violating my deep belief in what is safe. If I speak, it will probably be with timidity, and I will be overrun, will feel like a fool, and will reinforce my belief that political discussions are not safe. If I do speak up and survive, I will have stretched my comfort zone and changed my self-image just a little.

Figure 2
BALANCE SCALE

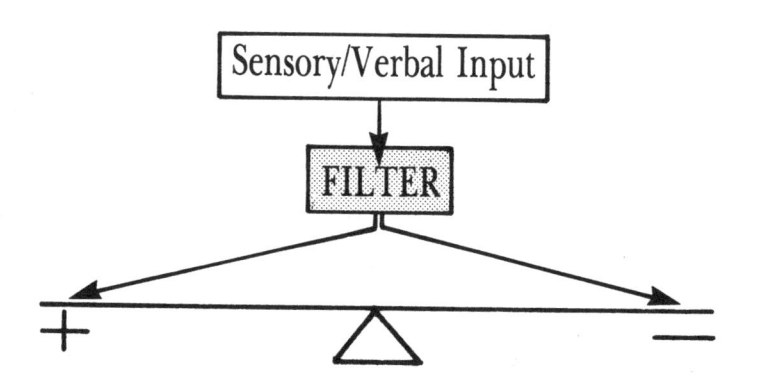

Each person's individual habits of filtering information determine whether a bit of input will land on the positive or negative side of that person's sense of well-being.

Controlling Our Filters

We don't know what is in our own filters, those associations that determine our responses, until we examine our own behavior. This filter can be gradually changed by accurate knowledge. We need to ask ourselves, "Why do I think that is dangerous?" (boring, desirable, etc.)—in other words, "Why am I judging this way?" We can change our filters by questioning our automatic responses and by feeding new information to our inner selves.

Sometimes a person walks away from work feeling slightly negative but not immediately able to identify why. Perhaps a woman, earlier in the day, had reveled in the brilliant leaves against the blue sky and seriously considered the idea of applying for a promotion. But now, only a few hours later, the day seems glum. The woman may find herself thinking, "I don't know why I thought I could apply for that promotion. I guess I'll just forget about it." Tracing back the change of attitude, she recalls the negative remark of a co-worker that had tipped the balance scale toward the negative. Her habit pattern has been to accept all critical remarks about herself as being true. However, by bringing the remark to conscious thought, she realizes that the criticism doesn't change her ability to do the job. Weighing the validity of the remark puts her in charge again and allows her to tip the scale back toward the positive. Without evaluating the remark, her confidence in herself would have been slightly lowered. The habit of checking the validity of what we allow to stay in our self-images is vital.

Making Changes

The Bible talks about our habits as our "ways," indicating that each person has habitual ways of responding to situations: the *way* of the sinner, the *way* of the righteous. In Psalm 119:1-2 the psalmist talks about people being blessed who *walk* according to the law of God and who *keep* his statutes. Walking and keeping imply habits—the habit of living life the way God ordained that humans operate best, as recorded in his "Operation Manual" for his creation: the Bible, God's message to us.

Our habitual choices result in blessed or unblessed ways of living. The Bible implores us to choose the good way, but that takes effort.

Exercise 2: Keeping the Status Quo

If you pursue the habits that currently run your life, what will you be like in five years?

1. In character?
2. In relationship to God?
3. In service to God?
4. In developing your gifts?
5. In relationship to your family?
6. In loving other people?
7. In effectively using your life?

Since we each choose the particular habits we want to keep or develop, we need to be able to identify areas we might want to change.

2

Habits Resulting from Fear

HABITS CAUSED BY FEAR HAVE A PARTICUlarly strong effect on our lives, particularly if they are developed before the age of seven. All habits of fear are restrictive and affect our choices and behavior. They restrict us by limiting us, inhibiting us, or causing us to become compulsive.

Limiting Habit Patterns: "Or Else!"

We were all taught certain fears as children, for our own survival or for our parents' comfort. These restrictions—"You *can't* . . . " or "You *have to* . . . "—were sometimes accompanied by a vague, undefined fear: the great *"or else."* When fear was excessively used (or we perceive that it was), the resulting habit nearly always has a limiting effect on our lives.

"Clarinda, don't you ever do that again, *or else!*"

Habits Resulting from Fear

Small children don't ask, "Or else what?" They simply fill their minds with dark, frightening images.

Some fears may be helpful in childhood but quite limiting for an adult. For example, the anxious parent of a child growing up near a dangerous cliff may have instilled in the child so much fear that the child grows to adulthood with an abnormal fear of heights or falling.

Inhibiting Habit Patterns: "Can't"

Most of us were taught that we *can't* go naked in public. The degree of repetition and the amount of fear used to keep us clothed determines how strong the habit pattern is for each of us. When all the guys jump into the pool naked and one little boy sits on the side with his clothes on, it is probable that his parents created great fear in him to instill the cultural expectation. That little boy may have avoided swimming parties all of his life, and at age forty may have difficulty getting into a jacuzzi with friends even in a swimsuit if he has not revised his restrictive habit pattern.

Children who have been put down in certain areas by being convinced that they *can't* sing, draw, tell a story, or throw a ball often go through life avoiding these activities. They feel too vulnerable to try the forbidden skill even as they grow older, and they remain too lacking in confidence to laugh about real inadequacies they may face.

Most of us have some inhibitions developed from fears attached to the word "can't."

The best way to deal with a "can't" is to ask yourself, "Why not?" Seriously consider doing the restricted activity unless it is physically impossible, illegal, immoral, or you realize that you don't want to do it. Then instead of "can't," why not say, "I *choose* not to do this because I don't want to" (or I am afraid or it's against my conscience). Accurate wording puts the action in the realm of choice and honesty rather than helplessness and excuses. It helps you take responsibility for your actions.

Exercise 3: Can't / Have To

1. Catch yourself every time you say "can't" and change the expression to "I choose not to."
2. Listen for the word "can't" in the conversations around you. Recognize the irresponsibility in that word.

Compulsive Habit Patterns: "Have To"

Compulsive patterns are developed from the "have to" admonition accompanied by fear of punishment, or especially fear of the unknown—the bogieman, God, and "or else." Some of us, even though overweight, still clean our plates because of a compulsion developed early; we simply cannot let food go to waste, even

Habits Resulting from Fear

though rationally we see the merit in limiting our intake.

We are unconscious of other compulsive habits because they seem so natural. In some families only *one right way* is allowed to set a table or load a dishwasher or store the hose. Everyone *has to* do the job that way only. Adults who grew up with the *one right way* may become anxious when that *way* is violated by someone. They may also become bossy and obnoxious.

The words "I have to" are almost always a lie. The most truthful "have to" that we commonly use is probably when we say, "I have to go to the bathroom," although even then there are alternatives. But most of the "have to's" we express are social excuses, not truth. "I have to go home to cook dinner." More accurate would be, "I want to get home because life is more pleasant if I have dinner cooked" (or I avoid a scene if dinner is ready, or I want to watch television and I'm using my family as an excuse). We hear people say, "I *have to* go to work . . . to school . . . finish this assignment." What people mean when they say "have to" is that they don't want the consequence of not doing those things. They are choosing to act in certain ways in order to achieve something they want or to avoid something they don't want.

Using "have to" also attempts to put the responsibility for our actions on someone else. To say "have to" implies that someone else is making us do something. Who is forcing us? What are the consequences if we refuse the "have to"? "I *have to* feed the cat" gives the impression that the person is slave to the cat's demands, when actually it's a desire to be a good person that results in the choice to feed the cat. Using "have to" is playing "parent" to oneself. We are trying to pretend that someone else can make us do what is right, as our parents used to do.

Once we recognize that we really have choices and that our "have to's" are ways to try to escape responsibility for ourselves, we are on the way to growing.

A "have to" statement may actually get done, but at twice the cost of effort. It may take more energy to overcome the muscle resistance to the words and the attitude that the words produce than it takes to do the chore. The term "have to" means that I am fighting myself or the imaginary boss who is making me do this.

Exercise 4: HAVE TO'S

1. List the "have to's" you have expressed in the past few days.
2. Reword each one to use "want to."
3. See if you can determine what responsibility you were trying to avoid in using the term "have to."

The Problems with Restrictive Habit Patterns

One problem with these restrictive habit patterns is that they make us less effective and

Habits Resulting from Fear

cause us to behave irrationally. For example, if being on time is a compulsive habit pattern, it may cause an otherwise good driver to risk crossing the railroad tracks in front of a train or running a red light or speeding recklessly because something unavoidable has detained him. The old "You *have to* be on time *or else!*" has blinded him to rational behavior. It also makes him anxious if someone else is late, so that he may ruin social occasions because he can't dissipate the anger caused by his anxiety. Or he may berate and nag the person who does not live bound by the same compulsions.

Some people with a compulsive understanding of male and female roles eliminate themselves from relationships with whole segments of the population because they are unaware of their limited thinking and the possibility of change. A woman may respond only to men who are flirtatious toward her. Her honest belief may be that men only want sex. Yet she is removing herself from friendship with men who regard a woman as a person rather than as a sex object.

Restrictive habit patterns create tension when they are in danger of being violated. A basketball player who has been convinced in early childhood that he *has to* succeed brings an added tightness to his muscles from this anxiety, which may cause him to fail. A singer who *has to* succeed may find her vocal chords tightening beyond the success level. Those with the inbuilt "can't" bring such anxiety to each challenge that, sure enough, they can't succeed.

Many of us burn energy needlessly fretting over the way other people do things. When someone else crosses a restrictive habit pattern of ours, we experience anxiety almost as though we had committed the restricted act ourselves. One woman became angry every time she used the community clothes dryer because the person before her hadn't cleaned the lint tray. Her "have to" was to clean up after herself, and her anxiety turned to anger when someone else did not conform to her pattern. When someone pointed out that she need only clean it once if she cleaned it at the beginning instead of the end, she was unable to accept that solution. She could not leave without cleaning the tray and continued to burn energy needlessly fuming about those who didn't have her compulsion.

"Buttons"

Whenever we feel ourselves uptight or anxious about the behavior of someone else, that person is probably offending one of our restrictive habit patterns. When we react strongly or irrationally to someone's behavior, it becomes apparent that we have vulnerable spots, or "buttons." When someone pushes a "button," our behavior seems perfectly rational to us but out of balance to those around. Buttons are part of the old, restrictive patterns that can be changed. We know we have buttons when we have anxiety over situations that others don't have, or when people are puzzled by our behavior. These overreactions cause us to be ineffective.

A fifth-grade teacher, unaware of his compulsion about waste, continually scolded his students if they threw away pieces of paper because they made one mistake. "Cross out, erase, and keep going" was his command. One day when a student crumpled up three sheets of paper in a row because she had made a mistake on the heading, the teacher became enraged, rescuing the rumpled paper, opening it up, and expecting the student to write on it. The student stared at him in shock.

"But it's my paper, not the school's!" she stated.

"I don't care," the teacher shouted. "You shouldn't waste paper!"

In describing the incident to a friend later, the teacher met with the same puzzled look. Finally it dawned on him that his anger had been totally out of proportion to the incident. When we are using too much energy on something not important, or not our responsibility, we probably are dealing with a button.

Some people's buttons show up internally. Children who were strongly impressed that they *can't* be angry or fight or stand up for themselves behave passively or cringe when they are attacked, thus bringing more attack upon themselves and encouraging the bully in others. The anxiety is internal and often causes physical damage to their bodies as well as creating debilitating life situations.

Even if you think the situations that upset you are important, the excess emotion you display indicates that your thinking pattern needs reevaluation and release from the emotional load. Awareness that this behavior is a button and that alternative ways of handling the situation exist is the primary means of ridding yourself of these unpleasant and irrational habits.

Exercise 5: Buttons

1. What are your buttons? List the situations that upset you, "set you off," or "burn you up."

Alternative Behavior

Another disadvantage of restrictive habit patterns is that they can blind us to valid alternative behaviors. The compulsive *(have to)* pattern closes the mind to any other way of doing something. When a friend suggests to a compulsive on-timer that "dinner at six" in some cultures means for people to start drifting in after six and dinner will actually be served about eight, the compulsive person doesn't want to hear about it. Even the discussion is upsetting. And he continues to serve dinner at his house at the given time, even if all of the guests haven't arrived.

The inhibitive *(can't)* habit pattern makes the victim unable to perform that one "can't" but leaves open all other possibilities. A person whose early childhood precluded ever eating with the fingers may be able to use toothpicks, napkins, tablespoons, chopsticks, knives, skewers—anything available to eat "finger food" as long as direct contact of hands and food is avoided. Recognizing these restrictive habits in oneself, acknowledging their limitations, and knowing that alternatives exist are essential to growth.

Victims of Our Fears

In addition to the fears taught us in our childhoods, we all have established some habits out of our own fears simply because there is much to fear in this new, strange world we entered as babies. These habits learned from fear may not be appropriate for us as adults.

Since the major work of life is overcoming fear, we need to eliminate some of the habits we formed in our childhoods when our fears were many. For example, if a person allowed a bad childhood experience with a cat to generalize into an attitude of dislike for all animals, the person is limiting his environment unnecessarily. Many of our social disabilities, such as mumbling instead of speaking clearly, retreating from new social experiences, and not saying hello for fear of not being answered, come from childhood shyness. All of these habits are inappropriate adult behavior that can be modified once a person recognizes the need for change.

Fear of change and fear of responsibility often combine to create a do-nothing pattern that shrinks and diminishes us.

Emily Dickinson puts it this way:

> The heroism we recite
>   Would be a normal thing
> Did not ourselves the cubits warp
>   For fear to be a king

Fulfilling the "kingness" in ourselves means extending ourselves for our own or someone else's growth or good—the opposite of maintaining the status quo, the opposite of inertia. We fail to stretch ourselves because of fear.

When fear takes hold, it limits faith, courage, risk, fun, potential, and eventually life itself. Each victory over fear—even a small step—moves us toward fulfilling the potential that God created within us. The habit of fear needs to be changed into a habit of trust in the One who created us and loves us.

One of the most repeated admonitions in the Bible is "Fear not." We are told in II Timothy 1:7 that God is not the author of fear but of power and of love and of a sound mind. Each fear released and replaced by trust strengthens the trust habit.

We are either increasing our habit of fear or increasing our habit of trust each time we are confronted with an opportunity to move ahead.

Exercise 6: FROM FEAR TO FAITH

1. List the fears that bother you or keep you from feeling free.
2. Now list a promise of God that can give faith or courage in the face of each fear. (If you can't think of any promises, you might try these for starters: Ps. 37:1-7; Ps. 139; Matt. 5:19-34.)

PROPERTY OF
SEYBERT U. M. CHURCH

PART TWO

Establishing New Habits

3

Motivation: Tool #1 for Building a Habit

ESTABLISHING A DESIRABLE NEW HABIT requires three steps: motivation, knowledge, and repetition. Without enough motivation, the habit is never established. Without knowledge of how to perform the habit correctly and how to fit it into one's comfort zone, one might establish a bad habit or fail in making change. And without consistent practice, a good behavior never becomes a habit. Motivation is the first key.

What is motivation? Motivation is an inner urge, a desire, that prompts a person to action with a purpose. Athough our minds and wills may both contribute to the forming and strengthening of desire, motivation is essentially an emotion. Two emotions motivate us, *want* and *fear,* and fear is the stronger of the two.

The Strength of Desire

The strength of the desire to form a new habit is the primary determining factor in how quickly and solidly it is established. One film at traffic school showing the blood and gore resulting from an accident in which seat belts were not worn could provide sufficient motivation to establish the seat belt habit. One burn from handling a casserole in the oven without a potholder may forge the potholder habit indelibly. Fear motivates because it increases desire—the desire to avoid pain.

In the above cases, the new habits don't require giving up something pleasurable, only a few seconds of time. No strong habit to the contrary impedes these new decisions. Therefore, motivation is strong enough, knowledge is sufficient, and all these new decisions need is regular reinforcement for a few weeks to be grooved into tentative habits.

An intense want mobilizes the entire body and mind. Since wants create aliveness, action, movement, excitement, intensity, and energy, discerning and feeling our wants is essential in order to have motivation for establishing new habits.

Exercise 7: Wants/Fears

1. What long-term wants do you have that are strong enough to cause you to sacrifice in order to achieve them?

Motivation: Tool #1 for Building a Habit

2. List other achievements or personal traits that you really want.
3. What fears do you have that could be used to provide motivational power?
4. What habits would be necessary to achieve these wants?

Willpower

Willpower is emotional power directed by the will. Sometimes we say that our willpower is weak. But willpower is neither weak nor strong; it is simply motivated or not. When our will (our decision-making power) is in line with our desires, we are likely to accomplish whatever we wish. The problem of failing to do what we have decided is not in lack of willpower but in the failure to check our motivations and to bring all of our desires in line with the new decision.

We all have experienced failure in trying to establish a new habit. These failures sometimes keep us from trying again because failure feels uncomfortable and we don't know how to try differently so that we can succeed. Our failures affect our self-images if we label ourselves as failures or even as people who are unable to accomplish that particular desire. Simply trying harder usually doesn't work. We need to increase our motivation.

But what can we do to make our motivation greater when we know a new habit would be helpful but we don't seem to be able to stick to the decision?

People—Help or Hindrance?

When two or more people agree on a want, it has more stability and power. Commitment to a like-minded person or group validates the desire and keeps the goal alive. This is why groups are helpful in establishing difficult habits. Alcoholics Anonymous and Weight Watchers show the power of group reinforcement to change habits.

Wants are undermined by doubting or nagging people. To expose a want to a person who will shoot it down—the pessimist—is dangerous, because it may dull the desire. To keep motivation strong, it is safer to share it with people who are encouragers and who basically have faith.

Words That Affect Motivation

As we have seen, the phrase "I *have to*" creates resistance in the body. The body automatically moves backward and the muscles tense. "Should" and "ought to" are indecisive terms. We usually follow "I should" with "but" and some excuse. "Ought to" is obviously a cop-out. "I need to" is neutral—not a positive motivator but not as much of a resister. "I choose to" signals accepting responsibility and a move toward the positive side. However, the only true motivator is "I want to."

To say "I should" or "I ought to" implies that I probably won't do it. Both of these terms create resistance like "have to," but with even less effect.

Motivation: Tool #1 for Building a Habit

"Should" and "ought to" make us uncomfortable, but we don't expect performance from ourselves. "Ought to's" and "shoulds" create the feeling that something is always hanging over our heads. Eliminating these two phrases from our vocabularies, along with "have to," frees us from a burden and makes us more honest. These words are energy-wasting guilt-producers, and we will be more productive people if we establish the habit of changing all the negatives to "want to's."

Placing "want to" in the wording of every purpose we expect of ourselves causes us to bypass resistance. The entire body cooperates toward the goal when we say, "I want to." Sometimes we don't feel honest in saying that we want to do something when we consider it a duty rather than a pleasure. However, part of us must desire it, or we wouldn't be trying to make ourselves perform this particular task. For example, when I say that I ought to write a letter to someone, where does the "ought to" come from? A part of my self-image must say that writing letters is a good thing to do. Since many people never think of writing a letter, the act has no inherent value—only the value we each give it. Therefore, if I would feel like a good person by writing a letter, I'm more likely to write it if I focus on my want. I *want to* feel like a good person, so I will write a letter. Of course, other acts would also make me feel like a good person. This broadens my options rather than limiting me to this one uncomfortable "ought to," so saying "want to" gets me in touch with a deeper part of myself than the surface "duty" person.

Exercise 8: Shoulds

1. List the "shoulds" and "ought to's" that you remember using in the past few days. Mark the ones that are important enough to change to "wants." Allow yourself to cross out all the ones that are not truly "wants." Feel the freedom in ridding yourself of those guilt-producers.
2. Take one item you have changed to "want" and record all of the reasons you want to do that. (For example, if your "ought to" list included visiting Grandmother, but many other activities have a higher "want" value, you may find that statements like these may raise the "want" value of visiting Grandmother:
   a. I want my grandmother to be happy, and seeing me would make her happy.
   b. I want my mother to stop bugging me about visiting my grandmother.
   c. I want to feel like a caring person.
   d. I want to go to a record store that is near my grandmother's house and could combine both visits.

The habit of using negative words creates a negative, non-growing person. Words like "can't," "have to," and "should" are not responsible words. They confuse issues, cloud reality, and delay decision. Two other irresponsible words are "always" and "never." When we become disgusted with ourselves, we may say, "I *always* lose my keys," or, "I *never* do things right." These are not true. The responsible act is to say what is: "I just lost my keys"; "I did this wrong."

When you hear yourself or someone else using negative words, a good response is "Sure enough!" meaning that the person using the negative has just limited his own options. If you say you can't, sure enough, you can't. If you say you "gotta," sure enough, you "gotta," (though of course you still might not). You have just locked yourself into your own self-fulfilling prophecy. Getting rid of negative words helps eliminate negative thinking. Responsible speech (I choose, I want, I did, I didn't) increases our alignment with truth and therefore makes us more like Jesus, who is the Truth.

When we are tempted to put ourselves down because we just failed to be what we want to be, a good phrase to use (and one that helps us visualize differently) is "That's not like me." For example, if Mary has just succumbed to a high-calorie dessert that she has been programming herself not to eat, she could say, "That's just like me; I always fail." Or she could say, "That's not like me," visualizing the new "me" she is trying to be. To change our self-images, we need to keep in mind the new creatures we are becoming and say to the old, "That's not like me."

Recognizing Conflicting Motives

To be powerful and stable, a want must be in tune with the whole person doing the wanting. It must agree with overall life goals, one's conscience, one's responsibilities, one's self-image, and one's dreams; otherwise, the motivation will be sabotaged by another aspect of one's life.

Many habits we would like to establish conflict with a previously comfortable pattern. Since the subconscious automatically strives to maintain the status quo, the conscious mind must intervene for change to take place. Thus motivation, which includes desire and decision, must be strong enough to overcome the comforts of the status quo as well as to surmount any existing motives that might be contrary to the new decision.

If the motivation for the new habit is an "ought to" or "should," the new habit is doomed. No power dwells in that motivation that can stand up to the power in the status quo. The "wants" of the new habit must be explored and reinforced or the old habits will hold.

To use the seat belt example again, if a person had heard a tale of someone being badly damaged by a seat belt, the conflicting fears could dilute the motivation for buckling up. Thus the new motivation to wear a seat belt must be strong enough to overcome the laziness of the status quo (no seat belts) and also the fear (motivation) that seat belts might be dangerous. Knowing the percentage of times seat belts save lives compared with the percentage of times that damage is done by a seat belt could increase the motivation to wear seat belts. New information can change motivation.

When we have conflicting desires, we need to examine our motives honestly and carefully. For example, a person may want to lose weight in order to look better in a new suit, but his social life revolves around food and drink—calories. By examining what food means to him (social comfort, reward, sensual satisfaction, or other emotional substitutes) and by becoming aware of what overweight means to him (safety from competition, an excuse for not participating in something undesired, or whatever else), he can see that the motivation of wearing a size smaller suit may not be able to compete at all with the motivation to eat.

If he cannot honestly tip the motivational balance—the emotion—in favor of limiting food, he may as well save himself the trouble of trying. His hope will not become a habit until his wants are all in line with the new goal. However, if a heart attack suddenly puts life and death in the balance, and losing weight is a means of staying alive, the emotional balance may tip in favor of fewer calories. Or, if he increases his knowledge of how weight loss could emotionally satisfy him more, motivation for the new habit might outweigh the old.

A person may want to add a thirty-minute quiet time to her morning rush. This would mean getting up a half-hour earlier, which would mean going to bed earlier, which would interfere with her social life. She has not only the status quo to fight, but the conflicting motivations of enjoying her social life and getting an adequate amount of sleep. She might be wiser to start with a ten-minute change.

Whenever we desire to establish a new habit that conflicts with a strong desire in the old pattern, we will not succeed unless we truly deal with all the motivations on both sides and our internal balances weigh heavier on the side of the new habit. Very strong desires stimulate creativity in reevaluating and reshaping parts of the life that conflict with this new habit.

Exercise 9: CONFLICTS

1. List the habits you have tried to establish without success.
2. Try to discern the conflicting motivation that prevented the new habit from being formed.

Visualizing the New Habit

We noted earlier that one way to turn around a setback in trying to establish a new habit is to say,

Motivation: Tool #1 for Building a Habit

"That's not like me." The primary way we can enhance our motivation is through our imaginations. When we can strongly feel in our mind's heart what we will receive from this new habit, we are hooking into motivation. For example, if a woman wants to change her response to a certain kind of situation, such as waiting three seconds before answering her husband instead of bursting forth angrily when he sets off one of her buttons, she can visualize herself reacting with this new composure in the same kind of situations where she normally would burst forth. When she sees her new self in her mind's eye and feels the new self in her mind's heart, she enjoys the pleasure of feeling in control of her emotions and she imagines the positive responses of her husband and children, thereby experiencing ahead of time the benefits of her new habit.

An important function that our imaginations play is to establish the first cobweb of a habit. It is hardest to do anything the first time, but if the imagination has done it again and again, the habit is already begun, and it doesn't feel like a first time when the act is actually performed in real life. Visualizing and feeling the new habit can increase our motivation for the desired change.

Emotion is far more powerful than reason in motivating us. The more pleasurable feelings we can put into our visualization, the more surely we will move toward the new habit. People trying to establish a pattern of putting things away may find it irritating to stop before leaving the room, the house, the yard, the car, to see if everything is shipshape. They may resent the time and effort it takes and think about how hard it is. Or they can visualize the pride and peacefulness they will feel when everything looks neat. They can imagine the freedom of being able to welcome an unexpected guest without excuses or embarrassment. They can feel the pleasure that will be theirs as they view each neat and orderly space. They can appreciate the efficiency of being able to find things.

People who focus on the difficulties rather than on the pleasure will probably never gain the habit no matter how much they try to force themselves. Those with the positive emotion have a good chance of forming the new pattern if no strong conflict interferes.

Vivid imagination is nearly the same as experience when the mind recalls it. Therefore, the aftereffect is also similar. Visualizing damaging things hurts us nearly as much as experiencing them, and visualizing ourselves as successfully accomplishing our good habits has nearly the same effect as practicing those good habits. We all visualize, sometimes "living" the movies or books we experience, sometimes becoming heroes of our own invention, and sometimes anticipating or "rewriting" real events. Visualization needs to be used very carefully.

When the motivators on the opposing side have been robbed of their power, it still is helpful to use the imagination to dwell on the good effects of having the new habit. Feeling pleasurable emotion when we visualize ourselves with the new habit established or with the effects of the new habit, such as a spirit of kindness rather than criticism, is part of the motivation. The more we visualize the positive effects of the new habit, the stronger the motivation becomes.

Exercise 10: VISUALIZATION

1. Choose a habit that you want to establish.
2. Lie down in a relaxed position.
3. Relax your body by letting go of all tension from toes to head.
4. Relax your mind by picturing a completely peaceful scene.
5. With eyes closed, look upward behind your eyelids until you feel close to sleep.
6. Picture yourself performing the chosen habit perfectly.
7. Feel the pleasure the new habit gives you.

Conviction to Do the New Habit

Another avenue to motivation is to become convinced. For example, if a preacher I respect tells me I ought to listen to God for twenty minutes every day, but I don't see how God is going to speak to me, I'm not likely to establish that habit. However, if that person convinced me that I would gain understanding of God, hear him speak to me, lose my anxiety, and begin to understand my gifts, I would undoubtedly try it. If nothing happened in a couple of months, I probably would drop it unless I was *convinced* that if I kept it up for six months all the good things would become true. *Convinced* is the key word, and conviction comes through knowledge.

When the motivation of the old pattern outweighs the desirability of the new, yet our minds discern that the new is better, a process of using knowledge to strengthen motivation can help. If a person who is trying to lose weight discovers that he feels hungry, but his stomach isn't empty, some facts may aid motivation. One, it's okay to feel hungry. Two, it may be gas; he can try burping. Three, it may be his mouth that is hungry, not his stomach; he can chew. Four, he doesn't need food; it's some other need that he's experiencing. Five, hunger pangs usually last only about twenty minutes. This knowledge can convince him to say no to his stomach and focus his mind on something else.

Exercise 11: CONVICTION

1. What habits do you want to establish but need more information about in order to be convinced?
2. Are they worth spending research time on?

Review of Methods to Increase Motivation

The first key to establishing a new habit is to strengthen one's motivation. Several means of increasing motivation have been presented. First, we recognize the power of people to motivate or hinder us. Second, we aid our bodies in conforming to the new habit by using "want" and "choose," while eliminating "have to," "should," "ought to," "can't," "never," and "always" from our vocabularies. Third, by knowing the motivations that conflict with the desired new habit, we can find better means of satisfying those needs, thereby robbing the old pattern of its power. Next, by using our imaginations to see and feel the desired results of the new habit, we can become eager to progress into the better way. And last, we can add to our knowledge about the good results of the new habit and become more convinced to make the desired change.

4

Knowledge: Tool #2 for Building a Habit

FORMING A GOOD HABIT TAKES CAREFUL planning and accurate knowledge. Since any habit that makes us more loving or responsible requires effort, we may as well take the time and energy to find out how the habit will be most effective. Two kinds of knowledge are necessary: (1) how to perform this new habit accurately, and (2) the process for forming this type of habit most effectively.

The Necessity of Accuracy

In learning tennis one can practice diligently, but if the racquet is held wrong or the swing is incorrect, all the practice in the world will not make an expert player, and the basics will need to be relearned correctly. Likewise, if a person is trying to overcome the habit of lusty language

Knowledge: Tool #2 for Building a Habit

but hasn't determined what substitutes to use for occasions that currently call for a forceful interjection, the language habit is unlikely to be changed. Diligently practicing new diet habits without checking their nutritional value may damage the body. Fervent prayer to a god of one's own making does not create a relationship with the Lord.

Gathering facts before starting on a habit change is essential. Knowing how the body works best to perform a physical task, knowing how the mind and emotions work to form an attitude or thinking skill, knowing how humans relate best to form a social skill, or knowing spiritual laws to form a spiritual habit is a pre-habit requirement to gain that particular pattern. It often saves time in the long run to spend weeks, even months, in gathering pre-habit knowledge.

The Tiny-step Process

Trying to make a major change in one's life all at once creates great stress because the comfort zone is stretched too far. When we choose major change, such as moving or having new people in our homes, or when we lose a place or a person or an activity that is part of our major comfort zone, we retreat to whatever comfort zone we have left and endure until our control panels adjust to the new environment. We are much more vulnerable to sickness and disease when our comfort zones are disturbed. So when we are creating the discomfort ourselves and the old comforts (habits) are still available, the temptation to drop the new habit is strong. Therefore, to be successful in changing habits, a basic rule is to take one tiny step at a time.

To reach an end, we must focus on the next step and make that our end. Even thinking about the later steps often interferes with the process of forming the immediate habit.

Character is built through a bundle of individual habits. Becoming a more godly person is accomplished by establishing the habit of regularly choosing a new action of goodness or kindness to work on as soon as the last is established, such as being absolutely honest in dealing with all the materials at work or consistently greeting each clerk you deal with. Without breaking down a generalized goal, such as being a better person, the goal will never be reached. But by choosing one tiny step at a time, that habit can be attained and another started. Progress in a particular direction is what is important.

Cues in Current Habits

Since habit is an automatic response to a cue, the first knowledge necessary for making change is awareness of the current habits that surround the area where a new habit is desired. What cue are you currently responding to at the time you want the new habit? Does a new cue have to be

Knowledge: Tool #2 for Building a Habit

established, or is a new response necessary to a current cue? Since more than 99 percent of our behavior is habitual response to cues, we most probably need to establish a new response to a current happening in our lives.

For example, we have routines that we follow when entering our homes. We place our coats and whatever is in our hands somewhere. If we are the people who can never find our keys and want to establish the habit of putting them in one spot, we need to first become aware of what our current habits are. Do we head for the mail? The bathroom? The refrigerator? The television set? What place is close enough to our usual paths to be acceptable? What cue can overcome the need with which we currently rush into the house?

A thorough knowledge of the activities preceding a bad habit helps us to see our current patterns of cue and response. For the key-loser, from the time the key opens the door until the hand puts it somewhere, the loser's mind is occupied with other needs and is not cognizant of the key. What cue could keep the key in his conscious mind until he places it appropriately? First, the person must clearly decide where he wants the key to be. Then, he must focus on taking the key out of the lock and gripping it until it is properly deposited. Eliminating interruptions between the time of taking the key out of the lock and putting it in the desired place will establish the habit more easily.

Hooking into an Established Routine

Establishing a regular sequence for all repetitive chores saves time, saves decision making that takes energy, and provides a framework into which new habits can be hooked. If your current repetitive routines are erratic, decide what order is most comfortable and stick to that sequence. For example, in the morning a person could turn off the alarm, go directly to the bathroom, use the toilet, the shower, the toothbrush, the deodorant, take a vitamin pill, go to the dressing room for clothes, dress, comb the hair, and head for the kitchen without making any decisions or even thinking. This automatic ritual frees the mind to plan other activities or to sing to God. It also allows one to work on several other habits that can become automatic.

Knowledge of existing routines helps one know where to plug in a new habit, since adding a habit is easier than changing one. In a well-established routine, each behavior cues the next one. Once a person recognizes how each ritual is a cue for the next, he or she can determine where to break into the pattern to add a desired habit. A church elder testified to adding a quiet time between showering and shaving. Since these were two strongly established acts that he regularly performed, he used the end of the shower as a cue to pick up his Bible instead of picking up his razor. Then, after his time with God, he picked up the razor and continued getting ready for the day.

Knowledge: Tool #2 for Building a Habit

Since morning routines are often the most clearly established, to add a clean-up habit to the morning pattern is easy. If turning off the shower usually cues a person to reach for the towel, he could reach for a wiping cloth instead and wipe the chrome and glass before reaching for the towel to dry himself. This is made easier yet if the wiping cloth is closer than the bathtowel.

Sitting at a table can cue one to pray. Walking through a doorway can cue one to look back and pick up what needs to be put away. Seeing a person can cue one to smile. Getting into a car can be a cue to be thankful. Hooking into an existing pattern is usually the easiest way to find cues for the new habits we want to add.

Exercise 12: Routines

1. List the sequence of your morning ritual and of any other times when you have three or more habits hooked together. This will provide places to consider hooking in new habits.
2. Establish a sequence if you lack one.
3. Identify spots where it would be possible to add a habit.

Preparation for a New Habit: Clothing and Equipment

Knowledge of all materials and equipment needed to perform the new habit accurately is another essential before trying a new habit. Clean-up tasks become habitual more easily if the material and equipment needed are available where the job needs to be done. Each toilet, sink, and tub needs its own material handy if clean-up is to become ritual. Having to go to the kitchen to get cleanser to clean the tub means it becomes a major chore. If bubble bath and cleanser are handy, the habit of cleaning after using is far more likely to be formed. Not automatically, of course; it still takes motivation, decision, and repetition.

Changing into the appropriate clothes for a task can be an added cue. If gardening after work is the desired habit, changing into gardening clothes and sitting in a chair that views the garden gets one in the mood. The clothing becomes an added incentive.

Preparation: Time and Place

Knowledge of our comfort zones, our needs, what motivates us, and our lifestyle patterns helps us determine the most effective time and place to plant a new habit. Perhaps the desired habit is to establish a reading time to review professional journals or prepare a Sunday school lesson. Certain places in the house cue us to relax. Some places are social; some places are more serious. To do serious reading, the area and the chair chosen must cue the mind to turn to serious matters. If the television set, the knitting, the

Knowledge: Tool #2 for Building a Habit

family, and the crossword puzzle are all available at the chosen spot, serious reading is unlikely to occur.

When an area becomes "contaminated" with social or recreational cues, doing serious work requires more energy. A young person's room is often the place for relaxation, phoning friends, music, and perhaps watching television—all social and recreational cues. To do her homework in that same place requires some cue that triggers serious thought. Adults can sometimes have one chair where only "thought" materials are available. This separation of place cues the body and mind that a different kind of activity will take place.

To establish the timing of habits also requires knowledge of oneself. To establish the habit of more serious reading or program watching requires giving up some lazier habits. At certain times of day the mind may need relaxation, something lighter. Knowing what your mind and body require at different intervals during the day will help in selecting the best time for a new habit. It also helps us discern laziness from rest.

Exercise 13: Preparation for a New Habit

1. Choose a new habit you would like to add to your life.
2. List any equipment, material, or clothing that would enhance this activity.

3. Decide the time of day and the place the new habit would most likely succeed.

Changing Self-image

Habits that are in keeping with our basic images of ourselves may be fairly easy to adopt. If one's self-image already says "I'm a neat person," adding a habit of wiping out the sink is in line with the basic image. Therefore, following the steps of motivation, knowledge, and practice will not be difficult.

The hard habits to establish are those that require us to violate our comfort zones. To establish habits that violate our basic pictures of ourselves, our comfort zones, requires a deeper change. We need thorough knowledge of the distance between the new habit and our current self-images. Then we need to decide on a tiny step that is in the right direction but is not too far away from the current comfort zone. A series of little steps will get us where we want to be more quickly than taking the big plunge.

Self-talk

We are all in constant conversation with ourselves. This ability to talk to ourselves (self-talk) gives us power to change the pictures we hold of ourselves.

One of the most important changes we can

Knowledge: Tool #2 for Building a Habit

make is what we say to our inner persons about ourselves. Any negative words we call ourselves, like stupid, clumsy, ugly, or "bad at . . . ," tip our inner scales toward a negative feeling about ourselves. These words have emotional power to make us feel bad. Then the automatic self-preserving mechanism makes sure that the negative image manifests itself in reality. We call ourselves ugly, so we feel ugly, so we act ugly, and our faces take on ugly expressions. Then, of course, we have proved to ourselves that we truly are ugly, and the image is reinforced.

Many of the words that came to us from our families were incorporated into our self-images. Where words conflicted, we intuitively chose those that were closest to the image we had already constructed. For example, if a child heard continually from his older siblings that he was clumsy, but an aunt told him how well he rode his tricycle, he might say to himself, "But I can't ride a bike," and cancel out the positive words.

Some of the images we hold came from experience—successes and failures, with the accompanying emotional impact of each. Since most learning in childhood is by trial and error, we experienced much failure. But the impact of our failures was individually interpreted by each of us according to what already resided in our internal images. In most homes children don't feel like failures when they don't walk perfectly the first time they take a step. Nor do most children stop trying when the first pucker of the lips doesn't produce a whistle. Trial and error implies that failure is part of learning.

Prenatal influences and genetic structure, our chemistry, and physical health all have had an impact. However, whatever our heredity and environment, as adults, even from the age of twelve, we are each responsible for our own self-images, and we must begin to get that image we hold inside ourselves in tune with the best potential that God has created in us. We have talents unexplored, minds not stretched, bodies not exercised, emotions hindering our joy, relationships undeveloped or hurting, and souls that haven't begun to understand life or God. By carefully screening the words we say about ourselves, we can begin to become the people we want to be.

Exercise 14: SELF-TALK

1. List all the words that come to mind when you ask yourself, "Who am I?"
2. After writing for two to three minutes, cross out the negative words and stop saying them even if you think they are true.
3. Read the positive words and feel pleasure in the pictures of yourself these words provide.

Knowledge: Tool #2 for Building a Habit

Affirmations

If our self-images now say, "I am a messy person," and we want to become neat, the first step is to visualize ourselves as neat people. To do that, we need to make a statement to replace the negative one. If we cannot visualize ourselves as neat people, then the statement "I am a neat person" is too big a step. We need to create a statement that is as close to the goal as we can visualize, for example, "I keep a neat car" (or whatever small piece of neatness is the first step). An affirmation needs to be positive, present tense, and emotionally pleasurable.

To be positive, the statement must be what you want, not what you don't want. "I am not messy" is a negative statement. It focuses on what we don't want. "I am neat" focuses on what we are moving toward, the new picture of ourselves. The affirmation also needs to avoid comparisons such as being better than or best. Comparisons are damaging because they put someone down. For example, "I am neater than my husband" puts him down and causes internal competition. Your job is yourself, not shaping up anyone else. Even to say "I am neater than I used to be" focuses on the negative and doesn't give a clear picture of you as neat.

Present tense sees ourselves as having already arrived. To say "I will learn to keep my temper" is like saying "I ought to or should." It is in the future and isn't becoming a reality. Present tense and personal—"I am . . . I give . . . I do . . . "—is the way to begin an affirmation.

Exercise 15: AFFIRMATIONS

1. Write an affirmation that is the next step for you in some area where you want to grow.
2. Practice writing affirmations for your thought life and your spiritual life.

5

Practice: Tool #3 for Building a Habit

ALL THE MOTIVATION, KNOWLEDGE, AND effort we put into establishing a new habit will not produce a habit unless we consistently practice it every time the cue occurs. Since habit is the *automatic* response to a cue, if we respond one way one time and differently another time, the response to that cue is mixed and does not become automatic. If one response is to the new and the other to the old, the old will win out because it represents comfort and therefore pleasure. However, each reinforcement in the desired direction works toward the point of automation if no other response is allowed. The first three weeks are the hardest.

Twenty-one Days to an Automatic Response

The responses in our neural system that forge a habit take about three weeks to become automatic. If the desired habit is to give thanks before each meal, the cue might be the act of sitting when a table has food on it. The desired response to the cue of sitting is to say thanks to God. At first we may need reminders—something out of the way to help us remember the cue. But if we are consistent, by the end of the third week the thought of thanks will automatically form in our minds. Then the effort to remember will be diminished greatly, and only the discipline to continue practicing remains.

Committing something to memory is a specialized kind of habit that follows the same pattern. To memorize information (a verse, a poem, history dates), repeating the selected material daily for three weeks will, for most people, establish it in the mind. A weekly review for the next year will make it yours for life, with only periodic reviews.

Defining the Cue

As the previous chapter indicates, choosing the cue is crucial. Adding a habit means choosing the right spot to fit it in. The cue is the activity you are doing immediately before the desired habit.

In eliminating a habit, the cue is established and the alternate response is what is needed. If a person wants to substitute grape juice for wine, the cue is reaching for the wine bottle. Then

Practice: Tool #3 for Building a Habit

choosing to reach for the bottle of juice rather than for the wine is the new and desired response to the cue.

If we find that the cue is too far removed from the response, we need to change the cue. For example, if sitting down at the table is often accompanied with much conversation, the habit of giving thanks might be difficult to practice. If this prayer is to be private, we might use the picking up of a fork as the cue. As we pick up the fork we hold it until we can utter a thank you.

Sometimes a cue becomes contaminated. The alarm is the cue to get up, but we have so regularly hit the snooze button that our response system says, "Alarm—snooze." For some of us, setting the clock ten minutes earlier and allowing one snooze time will work. For some, having the alarm across the room works.

If a cue stops working before we reach the fifth day, we probably need to change the cue or try a smaller step, something closer to the comfort zone. But if we can make it to the twenty-first day with only one or two relapses, the cue is becoming bonded to the response.

With some habits we want to establish, we may find that we don't arrive at the automatic stage even trying a second or third cue. When this happens, we need to review our motivation and knowledge tools to see what went wrong.

Exercise 16: FINDING CUES

1. List five habits you have and determine what the cue is for each. This will help you see the connection between cue and habit.

Internalizing a Habit

Remembering a new response to a cue may at first come too late. But each time we remind ourselves, the memory comes closer to the desired time. A group of teenage girls decided to eliminate certain slang words from their vocabularies. They chose substitute words that seemed less offensive to them and agreed to pinch one another if the undesired words were spoken. At first they said the old slang words without even a pinch. Then the pinches began. Soon they were catching themselves just after saying the words and would quickly say the desired expression. Then they would remember as they were uttering the wrong word and immediately substitute the right one. Next, the wrong words were only thoughts and provided the cue to utter the right ones out loud. In a short time, the desired words were coming out automatically. The process of internalizing a cue is to accept belated memory, correct the response as quickly as you remember, visualize the correct response as often as you think of it, and continue working closer and closer to the desired aim.

Practice: Tool #3 for Building a Habit

Exercise 17: REMEMBER SUCCESSES

1. Think of a habit you established in which you went through this process of remembering. This will help you be kind to yourself in establishing new habits.

Practicing Visualization

We have learned that visualization that is emotionally pleasurable moves us in the direction of that behavior. We can also get a head start on practice if we visualize ourselves responding in the desired way to a cue. If the desired new habit is to wait ten seconds and ask for wisdom before responding to a naughty child, we could visualize that practice before going to sleep. We would picture the child's wrong behavior and feel the calmness of waiting for wisdom, hear ourselves asking God for his perspective, see ourselves looking with God's love at that child, view ourselves responding with wisdom to the act of naughtiness, and see the child's behavior changing appropriately. Then in our visualization we would feel the joy of handling the situation in a productive way.

As we practice visualizing this new response to the cue of the child's bad behavior, we are forging a link between the cue and the ten-second prayer pause. The wisdom we receive as we visualize prepares us to receive the wisdom in the actual situation. The pleasurable emotion that we feel at the satisfactory resolving of the incident reinforces our desire to perform the new behavior.

Each time we plunge into immediate responses rather than practicing the new habit, we need to stop ourselves, take the ten seconds to move back into the new habit pattern, and change our responses in accord with the requested wisdom. If we don't remember the new response until after the incident is over, we can apologize to the child or simply say to ourselves, "Next time I will do this differently." Then we need to state or visualize what we will do next time.

The more often we visualize the new habit pattern with its accompanying pleasure, the more quickly we will establish the new habit.

Exercise 18: VISUALIZATION

1. Think of a habit you want to establish.
2. Define the cue.
3. Using the visualizing process explained in chapter 3, pages 54-57, begin with the cue and imagine yourself successfully performing this habit and enjoying the pleasurable results of it.

Exercise 19: STEPS TO ADD A HABIT

1. We are now ready to put the whole process together. Choose a small but

Practice: Tool #3 for Building a Habit

important habit you want to establish. Be sure that it is not far from your comfort zone, so that your first try is successful. Now follow these steps.

Step One: Decide what the new habit looks like. Picture exactly what you want. Be sure it is a small step.

Step Two: Think through (list) all the motivations that prompt you to develop the new habit. Visualize the pleasurable results.

Step Three: Gather all the information needed to ensure that the habit is being accurately performed. Acquire the material needed for successful accomplishment of the habit. Determine the time and place necessary for its performance. Visualize the accurate performance of the habit.

Step Four: Select the cue (the habit or happening that will precede and prompt the new habit) to be used only for this habit so that it can become automatic. Visualize immediately responding to the cue with the new habit.

Step Five: Write an affirmation that pictures the habit completed.

Step Six: Practice the new response every time the cue occurs and visualize it when you are at rest by using your affirmation.

Step Seven: Compliment yourself on each successful practice.

Additional Motivation

The forming of a habit involves reward. The steps of learning, according to John Dollard and Neal Miller, consist of drive, cue, response, and reinforcement (reward) (Calvin S. Hall and Gardner Lindzey, *Theories of Personality* [New York: John Wiley, 1957], p. 430). If the reward is not sufficient, the link between stimulus and response will not be established. Therefore, we need to determine carefully what reward we are receiving.

Obviously, the old responses to our cues are closer to our comfort zones than the new responses. And staying within that which represents comfort is rewarding. Therefore, the automatic system to maintain the status quo operates unless the emotional desire to change is stronger.

Some people reward themselves with something emotionally desirable, such as a food treat, buying something special, or going someplace special. These are temporary rewards, like playing good parent to ourselves, and can be helpful to some in the initial few weeks of attempting to forge the cue-response bond. Some people *deny* themselves something until a goal is reached. Giving up something for Lent in order to remember to focus on the meaning of Christ's

Practice: Tool #3 for Building a Habit

sacrifice for us is a motivation of this type. A person might give up reading mysteries or watching ball games until the three weeks of a new habit is established.

For some of us, simply reviewing the rewards of the new habit, reinforcing in our minds the reason that we chose to establish this new practice, can add the motivation that we need. If our inner structure doesn't truly believe that this new habit is more desirable than our previous laziness or alternate habit, we won't establish the habit.

Exercise 20: Rewards

1. List everything you can think of that would serve as a reward for you.
2. Cross out those that would in any way be detrimental to you.
3. Separate the remainder into two lists: those easy to obtain and those that require more time, money, or cooperation of others than would ordinarily be at your disposal.
4. Keep these lists as added knowledge of yourself for future use.

Breaking Old Habits

Similarly, breaking old habits requires that one discover the cue that prompts the habit. In the case of fingernail biting, usually the fingers touch the face or the thumb rubs over the nails. Becoming aware of these pre-biting cues is the first step in stopping nail biting. It is much easier to stop the touching than the biting. An alternative to the face touching is to occupy the hands with something else. Many cultures have worry beads, stones, or smooth pieces of wood that satisfy the need for touch and soothe one in tense situations. These are easy to carry. Another alternative is to grip something as soon as the cue occurs. It is easy to grip the arms of a chair or even one's own thighs without looking too peculiar.

The thumb rubbing against the other nails is often looking for a rough spot. Having a fine emery board handy and smoothing the rough spot also lessens the temptation of fingers in the mouth.

When the cue is emotional, such as emptiness, loneliness, frustration, or tension, finding a response that is acceptable to one's comfort zone and to the new image that one wants is difficult. However, by recognizing the emotional cue, the process of choosing alternatives has begun. When the response has been either mind-numbing (using alcohol or drugs, or engaging in promiscuity) or hyperactive (smoking, eating, or talking), a person may need a strong support group such as one of the twelve-step programs: Alcoholics Anonymous, Alanon, or Eaters Anonymous, for example. Many churches and counseling centers sponsor support groups. Habits that have created

Practice: Tool #3 for Building a Habit

chemical dependency usually need professional treatment.

Knowledge can be a powerful tool in breaking habits, both knowledge of the damage of the habit and knowledge of how emotional needs are met. Recognition of the cue is of high importance.

Exercise 21: BREAKING BAD HABITS

1. List bad habits you want to get rid of.
2. Check those habit changes for which you may need a support group. Choose one of these and check the phone book or ask your church staff, your friends, or a local counseling center for available groups.
3. Choose a bad habit you want to break on your own and follow these steps:

    Step One: Determine what cue(s) precede the undesired habit.

    Step Two: Choose one cue to work with. (If you can be successful in bonding one cue with a new response, you can work on each other cue one at a time.)

    Step Three: Decide on an alternate response to the first cue. When the cue that prompts the undesired habit occurs, what will you do instead? Picture the new response (habit) in detail.

    Step Four: Obtain whatever material you need for the new response (worry beads instead of nail biting, grapefruit juice instead of alcohol, nonfat yogurt instead of ice cream, gum instead of a cigarette, an uplifting novel to read instead of staying in a deep funk, etc.).

Step Five: List all the motivations that prompt the new habit. Visualize each reward with emotional pleasure.

Step Six: Visualize yourself performing the new response to the identified cue.

Step Seven: Write an affirmation that pictures the new habit successfully performed, and repeat it regularly.

Step Eight: Begin the new practice and continue visualization to reinforce the practice.

Step Nine: Compliment yourself on each successful practice.

Additional Knowledge

If the new cue isn't working but the habit seems to be desirable, searching for the conflicts may solve the problem. We can examine the alternate behavior to determine if it is just laziness or something more precious to the comfort zone. If the new habit desired is wiping out the sink after each use, and the cloth is handy, the thought to do it occurs, but we shrug off the thought and skip the desired habit, we are probably simply giving in to laziness. Recognizing the atrophy that accompanies laziness in any area of our lives may strengthen our motivation to push for the three weeks that it takes to reach for the cloth without consciously thinking of it.

Practice: Tool #3 for Building a Habit

However, what if the desired change of habit is to substitute chewing gum for chocolate, and the cue is the desire for chocolate, but after chewing gum the desire for chocolate continues. More gum, more desire for chocolate. Then we need to rethink the whole process. What does chocolate mean to our comfort zones? What is chocolate a substitute for? Perhaps our underlying need can be met in a more satisfying way than trying to change the symptom, and then the symptom that has become a habit can be more easily changed. With more knowledge of ourselves, we can sometimes structure the desired changes more easily.

Recognizing Emotional Needs

God has made us emotional beings and has provided healthy ways for our emotional needs to be met. He has offered us a relationship with himself that will meet our deepest needs, which no person or habit can fill. However, those who succumb to human nature's narcissism or laziness will never acquire that relationship.

Narcissism puts us and our wants and needs at the center of the universe, but a relationship with God requires that we acknowledge him as the rightful center and accept his ways, his truths, and our rightful subjection to him as bond slaves to Jesus Christ, whom God has announced is his Way.

Laziness robs us of that emotionally satisfying

relationship with God because it takes effort to know him. We must listen to his Word, walk in faith and obedience, and love those we don't naturally care about. This takes work. Laziness robs us of the emotionally satisfying life.

Habits of laziness are attempts to shortcut the process by which emotional satisfaction comes. When we feel an emotional drive or hurt and grab for an immediate gratification, we are attempting to bypass the work involved in real emotional satisfaction. One of the basic tools of life, according to M. Scott Peck, is learning to delay gratification (*The Road Less Traveled* [New York: Simon & Schuster, 1980], pp. 18ff). Practice of delayed gratification by sacrificing an immediate desire for a long-term goal in any area of our lives gives us the confidence that we can live satisfactorily without immediate gratification and may encourage delay in a harder area. Remembering our victories makes delayed gratification part of our self-images.

Exercise 22: EMOTIONAL NEEDS

1. List a habit that has been hard for you to break.
2. What emotional need(s) does this habit satisfy?
3. In what other ways could these emotional needs be met?
4. In what ways is your habit a product of laziness or narcissism?

Practice: Tool #3 for Building a Habit

5. In what ways is God the true answer to the emotional needs you are satisfying in this habit?
6. Now look at the cue that precedes the undesired habit and determine a constructive response to that cue which takes your emotional needs and God's answers into account.
7. Visualize the new response to the old cue; obtain any materials needed for the new practice and rid your environment of any temptation to the old; begin the new practice, continuing to visualize both the process and the pleasurable rewards you will obtain.

Relapses

During the first three weeks we need to be as consistent as possible in linking the cue with the desired response. However, we need to be pleased with ourselves for every day that we are consistent. If we have three days of reinforcing the new habit and then miss a day, we can take a little time to visualize doing the new habit perfectly in order to make up for the break in the pattern. We can ignore the failure and set our minds to pursuing the new habit.

Anytime we respond incorrectly to a cue, we can give up or we can reinforce our desire for the new habit and keep going. When we put ourselves down, give negative messages to ourselves, or quit trying, we groom ourselves for failure. Messages we give to our self-images, such as "I can't change," "I'll never be able to establish this habit," or "I always fail," are excuses we give ourselves to justify not trying. They are also lies. Words such as "can't," "always," and "never" are exaggerations and lead us to believe ourselves to be weak and helpless victims. We are not victims unless we choose to be by our careless language and laziness.

If our cues are well selected, our motivation is certain, and our knowledge is accurate, two things will help us in a relapse. First, we can visualize success to counteract the relapse. Second, we can say, "Next time," and decide exactly what we will do the next time the cue occurs.

It may take longer than three weeks for the pattern to become automatic, but as long as we are moving in that direction, there is no need to give up.

Exercise 23: WHEN THE OLD RESPONSE CONTINUES

1. Reexamine the cue and your choice of an alternative response.
    a. Is the step too big? See if you can find a smaller step where you can achieve success.
    b. What is there about the old response that is more satisfying? Use information

Practice: Tool #3 for Building a Habit

(self-talk) to diminish the pleasure of the old and increase the satisfaction of the new.

c. Can you increase your motivation for the new response by dwelling on your desire for the new habit, by acknowledging the fear of what will happen if you don't form the new habit, so that the new response is more desirable than the old? If you can, try again. If not, look for a new alternative response to the cue.

2. Focus on why you want to change the habit. Are your motives in line with your whole self? Do you have a more important habit you need to be working on? Would achieving the new habit make your inner self feel unsafe, compromised, stretched too far, or uncomfortable for any other reason? If so, would it be wiser to focus on a different step of growth at this time?
3. Have you thought through all the steps of the new response to your old cue carefully? Have you visualized each aspect?
4. Success breeds success. Be sure that you have succeeded in adding or changing a small habit before you tackle a major area of your life where you have felt failure.

Times to Be Wary

Every time we go on vacation; someone visits; we have a change of job, home, or housemates;

sickness occurs; or any other out of the ordinary experience intrudes upon our good habits, we need to take special care to reestablish them immediately upon return to normal. It takes very little effort to pick up a habit that has been temporarily dropped, but much effort to start over after strongly establishing other patterns from the default system of laziness. Wisdom dictates that we evaluate and make decisions about our habits every time change occurs in our lives.

PART THREE

Choosing Habits for a Lifetime

6

Relating Our Habits to God

THE PURPOSE OF OUR HABITS DETERMINES what changes we will make. If the primary habits we want to change are our eating habits, our exercise patterns, or some other physical habit, what does this tell us about our goals? Is our major concern appearance? Health? Social acceptance? What about our souls, our minds, our ability to love, our responsibilities as part of God's creation? Aren't these non-physical habits equally important—perhaps more important—than the body? The internalized goals of our hearts may be possessions or power or fame, security or belonging or romance. Or we may be closed down, living in depression or idleness. Most of us have vague, temporary goals and go through a period of depression every time our goals are finished. The "empty nest" syndrome can hit men and women whose only focus has been parenting; early death after retirement can hit those whose primary focus has been their job.

No matter what we say our goals are, our behavior will follow what is deeply internalized in our comfort zones. If, in observing our own behavior, we see a discrepancy between what we think our goals are and what we see in our actions, the way to make change is through affirmations, clearly visualized and regularly fed into that inner control panel.

Life Goals

We need to *know what we want*. Since wants are the only motivation we have other than fear, we are wandering in the dark if we do not clarify our desires and focus the direction we are headed. We do this by stating and internalizing a few simple lifelong aims.

A life goal needs to be an interest that continues until death and is never finished, but has triumphs along the way. Paul the apostle's goals were mentioned throughout his letters. One was to "press on toward the goal for the prize of the upward call of God in Christ Jesus" (Phil. 3:14). Another was to "know him [Christ] and the power of his resurrection . . . share his sufferings, becoming like him in his death, that if possible I may attain the resurrection from the dead" (Phil. 3:10-11). Both of these are general goals that any Christian could adopt.

Paul also had a goal unique to himself: He was the apostle to the Gentiles. This he expressed in his letter to the Romans; he was called and set apart "to bring about the obedience of faith . . . among all the nations" (1:5). We each need to know our own gifts and callings sufficiently to want to be or do that which is unique to ourselves, in addition to the goals that every Christian has.

Life goals need to be broad enough to never be totally finished, yet they must have pieces along the way that are attainable. They also need to be in tune with the good, that is, with what God is working toward in the world. Life goals need to be beyond ourselves, yet specific enough to enjoy pursuing. An entertainer's life goal might be to help people laugh, or it might be to gain fame by performing. When the entertainer no longer gets gigs, she can still pursue the first goal by making the people around her laugh, but she may become bitter if she still seeks the world's applause. Likewise, a craftsman's goal may be to produce and appreciate beauty, or it may be only the praise he gets from his products. When his hands are no longer steady, he can encourage and appreciate the skill in others if his goal is to appreciate as well as produce, but if production is his only goal, he will feel useless.

We each need to clarify one or two life goals that will keep us from falling into the trap of laziness or narcissism. The natural state of elderly people is to turn inward and focus only on themselves. The antidote is to have conscious goals that keep us focused on God and his work, which is to love people and fight evil.

Choosing Life Goals

People who have no life goals are scattered, living from emotion to emotion; those who are not pursuing their life goals are squandering their time and energy on inconsequential matters; those who have the wrong life goals are wasting their energies on useless or even damaging behavior.

Without a life goal that is in line with God's purpose for us, we have no basis on which to make decisions. Confusion is common, and depression is normal each time that a temporary goal is met. God has given us principles and commandments out of which we are responsible to determine our life goals.

First, God's commandments are summarized in Matthew 22:37-38: "You shall love the Lord your God with all your heart, and with all your soul, and with all your mind. This is the great and first commandment. And a second is like it, You shall love your neighbor as yourself." In keeping with this statement, the Shorter Catechism (Presbyterian) states in answer to the question of our purpose or goal: "to glorify God, and to enjoy him forever." Our life goals need to include the concepts of loving, glorifying, and enjoying God.

In choosing life goals, we can consider several aspects of the two great commandments. One of the evidences of loving a person is to want to be like that person. We desire to be like God, and

God desires that we be like him. To be like God we must keep looking at him so that in time we will reflect him. Therefore, one way to love God is to focus on him by meditation, praise, reading his message to us (the Bible), and participating in group worship.

Another evidence of loving a person is to desire what they desire. The second commandment tells us that God desires that we love our neighbors. As we become like Jesus, we will become loving people, but we have more clues to God's desires for the world in the prayer Jesus gave to his disciples, found in Matthew 6:9-10:

> Our Father who art in heaven,
> Hallowed be thy name.
> Thy kingdom come,
> Thy will be done,
>   On earth as it is in heaven.

The Shorter Catechism interprets the first three petitions to mean that God wants his name to be made known; that he wants Satan's kingdom destroyed and God's kingdom advanced, with others brought into it; and that he wants us to know, obey, and submit to his will in all things. To want what he wants is to continually refine our knowledge of his will, to work with him to overthrow Satan's holdings and establish the kingdom of God, and to long for the whole world to acknowledge his glory. These goals will align us with God's purposes.

Our life goals need to be both general (to glorify God and enjoy him forever) and personal (reflecting our own piece of the action). We each reflect God in a particular way and are endowed with specific gifts to accomplish God's plan in our corner of the kingdom.

To avoid scattering our minds' energies wastefully, we need to clarify our life goals. These are general purposes rather than specific time-oriented objectives. For example, if one of my life goals was to seek and communicate truth, this would still be going on until the day I die. An objective along the way might be to write a book on a particular topic or to teach a class to communicate some truth God has impressed upon me. Objectives to further the goal that can be completed in a reasonable time-frame keep the goal alive and exciting. But life goals need to be broad enough to keep us motivated until death. By establishing our life goals so firmly in our conscious minds that they seep into our subconscious, we filter all of our attitudes and interpret all input in accordance with these goals.

Exercise 24: LIFE GOALS

1. In what issues or directions has God endowed you with gifts, prompted you, compelled you, or interested you?
2. What do you want to be working toward until you die?
3. What does Scripture tell you that God's purposes for you are?

4. List your life goal(s).
5. Put them in the form of affirmations and repeat them daily.

Sample Affirmations:
> I am glorifying God with my heart, mind, and soul.
> I love God with all my strength.
> I press toward the prize for the high calling of God.
> I am created to seek truth and communicate it lovingly.
> I am called to bring justice to the poor.
> I am ordained to preach the good news to all who will hear.

Habits of Loving God

If our most important job in life is to love God, then our habits need to reflect that love. When we love someone, some of our most meaningful moments are in telling them of that love. Praising God and thanking God are elements of expressing our love, but why not say, "I love you, Lord"?

Some of us grew up in families that didn't express love verbally, and we may find it hard to say, "I love you." The first time I heard an elder pray aloud the words, "We love you, Lord," I was embarrassed, which gives evidence of my restrictive habit patterns. However, now I enjoy the focus on God as an object of love which that statement gives.

Change Your Bad Habits for Good!

Many religions have a mantra or repeated phrase that is used to focus the mind. A number of Americans, even Christians, paid money to receive a mantra in the days when Indian gurus were popular. This was a syllable that they repeated to help them empty their minds in order to focus and meditate.

Each of us has a name at the bottom of our souls that is our cry in time of intense fear, joy, or success. For children, it is usually "Mommy" or "Daddy." For adults, it may be the name of the spouse or a child. But for many adults, the cry is "God," and we each have our special names we use for God.

Christian meditation is not mindless; therefore, our repetitive phrases are words that focus our minds. The repetition of Hail Marys and Our Fathers that Roman Catholics use can provide that quieting, centering function. The early church had a Jesus prayer that was a simple statement of who Jesus is. Bible verses can be used to aid our awareness of God and fulfill his command for us to love him. Phrases or choruses from a hymn or a spiritual song are easy to repeat or sing in the car, while doing dishes, when alone in the house, or when walking outside. Some people repeat the Twenty-third Psalm in times of fear or distress. We need to choose a phrase that expresses our love for God, choosing the name for the Almighty most precious to our own hearts, and determine cues (such as seeing beauty, hearing sad news, driving down a particular street, entering the kitchen) that will prompt us to repeat that statement of love.

The repetition of our love for God as a habit focuses our hearts on the single most important goal of life.

Habits of Praising God

Our chief end is to glorify God and enjoy him forever. Praising God is one means of glorifying him. In praise we name his attributes, reminding ourselves and glorifying him by remembering all the aspects of who he is.

Memorizing hymns of praise that list his names, such as "Immortal, Invisible, God Only Wise" or "Fairest Lord Jesus," is a helpful means of establishing the habit of praise. Then we can sing or recite his attributes at will.

Memorizing portions of Scripture, especially from the Psalms or Isaiah, allows us the habit of praise wherever we are. Isaiah 40–44 is particularly rich in poetic expression of God's greatness.

Habits of praising God begin with cues. What are the daily and weekly activities that we will establish for praising God individually and corporately?

Exercise 25: Habits of Loving God

1. Write your love-phrase to God.
2. List the praise psalms, hymns, or verses that you know or plan to memorize.

3. Determine the cues that will prompt you to express your love and praise of God.
4. List where and when you will worship God corporately with his people.

Sample Affirmations:
 I love you, Jesus.
 Father, I adore you.
 I praise you, Almighty God, Everlasting Father, Prince of Peace, my Rock, my Refuge, my Redeemer, my Hope, Counselor, Shepherd, Healer, Savior, Comforter.

Habits of Listening to God

Do we love someone if we never listen to that person? As in any relationship, if time is not set aside for communication, the relationship doesn't grow. If people are simply coexisting without sharing and listening, love deteriorates. Jesus says that if we don't hear him, we are like stony ground where the seed that could grow to great richness is washed away. Listening expresses our interest, our respect, and our love. We listen to God first by reading the letter he has sent us, and second by being quiet to hear what his Spirit is saying.

Having a daily time to communicate with God is essential to spiritual growth. Three elements are essential: listening, responding, and sharing/asking. First, we listen by examining what he is saying in the Bible, his message to us. We must read deeply, by meditating on individual verses and phrases, and broadly, by covering the whole Bible every few years, so that we see who God really is, not just keep imaging him in our favorite way.

We respond by applying what he says to our lives, so we need to ask the questions, What is he saying to me? What does he want me to do? But we also need to see the variety of ways in which he reveals himself in the sixty-six different books he has given us. The same God interacted with humans in Genesis and Revelation, in Job and John, in Habakkuk and I Peter. We need to see him in his various manifestations and his dealings with all kinds of people through the various eras of humankind. Therefore, finding a system to get through the entire Bible periodically is important. Reading through in a year takes about a half hour of steady reading per day. To be realistic, most of us would aim for two or three years to complete the course, or find courses at church that would provide this breadth.

Not only do we need to know what he requires of us, we also need to continually ask, What have I learned about God? If we don't have questions about God, we aren't growing in getting to know him. Our culture's image of God is greatly skewed from his revelation of himself in the Bible. Our response may be disbelief, anger, dislike, or fear, but acknowledging our responses to what we see of him in the Scriptures is an essential part of listening to God. Who he is is the most important factor in our lives. It helps some people to write down their responses: what he says, what they think, what they feel, their questions—even if they don't know the answers.

The third aspect of communication is to share with him the other concerns of our hearts and again listen for what he tells us about these concerns. Sometimes it is hard for us to listen, especially when we are locked into our own answers. Many times we try to make God our personal puppet by demanding that the Almighty give us exactly what we want on our own terms. Sharing our concerns means acknowledging our needs, frustrations, cares, and desires, and asking for what we want. We are instructed to cast all our cares upon God. Then our job is to listen to the creative alternatives the Spirit may suggest and to trust in God's means and time.

Structure is helpful to establish the habit of listening. A special place that is used only for holy, or at least serious, pursuits will help you focus. Being alone is ideal, even if it means getting up earlier or leaving the family in pursuit of television. Your Bible, hymnbook, notebook, and pen need to be handy. If the time is the same daily, the mind anticipates the desired attitude.

When other thoughts continue to barge in, it helps to deal with them. One way is to hold your hands palm up on your lap. Then visualize in your hands the first person or problem or possession you need to deal with. Lift your hands

Relating Our Habits to God

up as though giving the object to God. Ask God, "What are you doing in this situation? How does he [she/it] fit in with your grand plan? What do you want?" Then listen. Jesus says, "No longer do I call you servants, for the servant does not know what his master is doing; but I have called you friends, for all that I have heard from my Father I have made known to you" (John 15:15). God wants to share with us what the Godhead is doing. When the Shepherd has quieted your heart and let you know your role, let God take the burden and dispense with it as he wants.

We tend to limit our communication with God in several ways. Some of us don't ask enough. We go through life oblivious to our needs or God's desires, or we are fragmented because our focus is not on God. God tells us to ask, for in asking we get in touch with our own desires and with God's plans. Some of us don't listen. Our prayer lives consist of reciting lists of complaints or requests to our personal "puppet," telling him how to run the world rather than having a conversation with him about his interests (what we read in the Word) and our concerns. And of course, some of us won't listen because we are afraid that God won't give us what we want. We refuse to trust that his love will give us the best because we are so sure that we know what best is.

Exercise 26: Quiet Time

1. What is the time and place of your daily communication with God?

2. What plan do you have for listening to his whole message—all of the Bible?
3. What will help you to make the time a real communication between two who love each other?
4. What information, material, changes, cues, and decisions do you need to make this work?

Habits of Trusting God

Faith is the habit of trusting God. It is not a feeling. The old tale of three children walking across a log exemplifies what faith is. The first child, Fact, was certain that the log was sturdy and wide enough for the three to cross easily. He showed the others how much wider the log was than the path they were on. He helped them examine its surface to see that it wasn't slippery or uneven. Then Fact said, "Follow me." Faith was the second child. She kept looking at Feeling, who was behind her, to determine what to do. Fact said, "Just keep your eyes on me and Feeling will follow." So Faith stepped on the log, keeping her eyes on Fact, and Feeling followed right along. Faith is based not on feeling but on truth.

When we know a truth of God and act on it without hesitation, regardless of our fear, we are establishing the habit of faith. Life is difficult, and God didn't promise to make it easy; he just promised to be with us. Change is difficult, but no growth occurs without change; our faith is that

Relating Our Habits to God

God is with us. God does not give us a detailed map of life; he gives us principles and a brain. If we make a foolish decision, he is with us and is the one person who doesn't condemn us. He is not concerned with our efficiency or our avoidance of mistakes or even our success in a given project; he is concerned with our growth. Therefore, we are free to fail. Abundant life is not lived statically or remaining in the status quo. The more we reach out in service and love, the more God increases our faith.

An evidence of faith is thankfulness. The habit of thanksgiving is strongly recommended in the Bible. When we give thanks, we focus on the beneficial side of an experience. We could criticize the same experience, and some of us have overdeveloped critical faculties. But unless we are in a position to make change, criticism almost never helps. Thankfulness helps us and others know what is good, what to repeat.

A thankful attitude does not mean being dishonest. We are not thankful for the evidence of sin in the world, such as disease, war, and injustice. But we can be thankful for God's presence with us and his work in making change toward life, peace, and justice.

Throughout the Bible, God had his servants list the specific things God had done so that they would remember his power and care. Festivals such as Passover and Jubilee were established to remember his love toward them. We now have Christmas, Good Friday, Easter, and Pentecost to recall Christ's intervention in the world. We need to make our own lists of miracles, blessings, and special communications from God to remind us of his work in our lives. Thanking God is a means of entering God's presence.

Exercise 27: FAITH

1. Make a list of events in your life that you are thankful for.
2. Establish a time every day to say thank you to God.
3. Decide one risk that you could take to encourage the attitude of faith in yourself.

Being Transformed by the Way We Think

Paul encourages us to be transformed by the renewing of our minds, that we might prove what is that good, acceptable, and perfect will of God (Rom. 12:2). When our goal is to glorify God and be like him, our habits gradually mold us to his image. Our minds are renewed as we see God more and more clearly, as we see ourselves more and more as the Lord sees us, and as the Holy Spirit increases our desire to be all that we were created to be.

If a young woman's grandfather had been a multibillionaire, and he had set up a trust fund for her to have any kind of education she desired and to be able to begin any business she wanted, her behavior would be affected in many ways. Her plans, her manner toward other students, her regard for work, her expectations of lifestyle, her view of marriage, her choice of college courses, and her interest in the world all would be affected by her knowledge of who she is—a person born to wealth with unlimited options for education and business.

If I knew that I were the daughter of a powerful ruler, that I had been appointed to rule with him, that I was expected to build the character necessary to be a good ruler, that I had been given certain ambassadorial roles to accomplish during my training years, that I had been given information and power to accomplish those tasks, that I was one of many siblings assigned to their own tasks toward the same goal as mine, and that I could have a private audience with this powerful ruler at any time I wished and ask for whatever I wanted to accomplish the assigned tasks, every aspect of my life would be affected.

I would carry myself with authority. I would interpret my circumstances in the light of the current tasks I had been assigned and the future rule I was destined for. I would be inferior to no one, but in keeping with my ruler's desire for my character, I would be superior to no one. I would act with purpose at the smallest task required because it was part of the overall plan for my good. I would be confident that he had enough resources for me to continue my work and training indefinitely.

The above is, of course, true. I am a daughter of God. This knowledge of who I am is basic to my self-concept. Whatever else I am by my genetic heritage and my environment, this knowledge of who I am in God supersedes. We all need to affirm who we are in order to get our self-concepts in line with truth and reality.

The most basic truth that determines our characters is the knowledge that God loves us, because our capacity to love is limited by how much we perceive that we are loved. The largest portion of one's character consists of the ability to extend oneself for the spiritual growth of others, which is love. We can do this only to the extent that we feel valued and loved ourselves. No one experiences perfect love from another human being since we are all too needy to love completely. Therefore, our willingness to let ourselves feel loved by God, who alone can love perfectly, governs the potential to which our characters can grow. Every thought that builds the habit of feeling loved by God helps lay the foundation on which character is formed.

Exercise 28: Totally Loved

1. In what ways would you be different if you wholeheartedly believed that God joyfully created you, tenderly watches over you, and yearns for your best?

Relating Our Habits to God

Accepting Ourselves

When we accept who we are before God, we have the beginning of an accurate self-image. I am a creation of God, given purpose by his call. I am loved by God, redeemed by his grace, chosen to be his child and heir, promised a position reigning with him in eternity, forgiven every sin, empowered by the Holy Spirit, indwelt by his love, and have available his joy. These are but a few of the truths that I can let seep into that picture I hold of myself.

Because we were born into a fallen world with self-centered natures, the self-images we all start with are warped by varying degrees of fear and misinformation, which God's grace intends to change. The more we dwell on the truths of who we are in God—safe, loved, protected, given purpose, granted eternal life, expected to work at doing right, and expected to work at loving—the more quickly our warped views will come into line with God's image of us.

Although God never promised us an easy life, if we absorb the truths that he has given us, we will have a joyous life, now and in eternity.

Exercise 29: Affirming Who I Am

1. Select three words that are most emotionally satisfying about who God says you *are*. Write these in a short, positive sentence.

2. Repeat the sentence over and over as you go to sleep, as you wake up, as you are driving, when you feel happy, and when you feel afraid.
3. Picture and feel yourself receiving these gifts from him. The emotional impact of the picture, the feeling, and the repetition of the words will seep into your self-image.

Sample Affirmations:
    I am loved, forgiven, and chosen.
    I am a daughter of God, joint heir with Jesus Christ, and abiding in his love.

Affirming Truth

The process of affirming yourself with positive truths will gradually change your image, of course, since we become what we picture. If you find yourself short-tempered one day, or clumsy or forgetful or rude, to dwell on these characteristics is to reinforce them. Instead say, "That's not like me," because that is not like the new creation in Christ that you are becoming.

Remember to picture in your mind the situation in which you were not the person God intended you to be and picture (feel) yourself responding the way you want to respond next time. You will put a positive image in your mind and be prepared for better behavior next time. Vivid imagination equals memory, and every behavior leans us toward a habit. To let the wrong behavior go without acknowledging to God and yourself that it was wrong and determining what is right for next time is to move toward a bad habit rather than a good one.

The habit of reviewing the day and revising bad behavior into "next time" behavior keeps that old self-image growing positively.

Jesus says that what the mind dwells on the person becomes (Matt. 6:22). In interpreting that passage, Paul Byer (of the Inter-Varsity Christian Fellowship) says that what the eye is focused upon fills the vision and becomes the primary concern of the body. We certainly don't want to dwell on ourselves all the time, but since some of our thoughts do focus inward, especially when we are dissatisfied with our behavior, we need to be sure that our thoughts are in line with the truth that God has expressed in his Word: that we are loved, forgiven, gifted, and empowered to grow in righteousness and love.

Inner Healing

Some people have self-images that have been badly damaged because of the sinfulness of the world in which we live. Their prenatal and early childhood experiences may have given them the belief that they are unlovable or incapable. Their filters are full of lies about themselves and the world, the greatest lie being that they are unlovable. For the truth of God's love to seep into their damaged perception will take healing. The truth of God's love for them may only come through being accepted into a loving community.

Prayers for healing can be a source of allowing God's love to seep or zap in. Psychotherapy in a loving therapist/client relationship can be helpful in sorting out lies from truth. But above all, a regular caring relationship with loving Christians is God's way of healing.

Eliminating Comparisons

One attitude that defeats us is our tendency to make comparisons. Comparisons are damaging; either they make us feel superior to someone or inferior to someone. Neither superiority nor inferiority is healthy. God has made each individual beloved and useful to him. An intelligent child growing up in the shadow of a brilliant older sibling may perceive himself as dumb, even though his brainpower may be superior to that of most of his peers. Whatever he does, he will never be able to compete successfully with older brother. But the comparative perception is not a true picture of his ability.

Because of our comparisons, our competitions, and our insecurities, we misinterpret reality. We all have areas where our perception has been inaccurate. The physically handicapped person may feel incapable when comparing herself to a walking or hearing or sighted person. But she is capable of performing God's task for her. She may rebel against what that task is, but in accepting her role in God's kingdom she can find joy and completeness. Comparisons are deadly. Even comparisons of your church, your house, your pastor, or your school with others usually leaves someone feeling put down or suspicious that you're going to put them down the next time. Comparisons not only hurt, but the person who makes comparisons makes other people uncomfortable.

Exercise 30: POSITIVE-SELF PICTURES

1. List all the positive aspects of who you are without comparing yourself to anyone else.
2. Picture each statement, allowing yourself to feel the pleasure of being each image.
3. Choose the two or three mind pictures that give you the most pleasure and make copies of these statements to put in places that will remind you of who you are.
4. Dwell on these pleasurable pictures before sleep when your subconscious is most receptive to remodeling your self-concept.
5. Whenever you start comparing yourself to others, stop and state a positive, true fact about yourself.

Sample Affirmations:

I am lovable, capable, intelligent, and kind.
I am godly, hardworking, and loving.

7

Habits of Thinking

Plutarch says in *On Moral Virtue, IV,* "Character is simply habit long continued."

Just as our feet make pathways when we walk and our bodies respond habitually to certain routines, so our minds form ruts of thinking. To the extent that these patterns conform to reality as God has made us and contain the essential truths of God, the mind is healthy. If the thinking patterns are filled with falsehood or frivolity, the mind lacks health. Since these deep beliefs of the mind become attitudes and set the tone for our emotions and behavior, our entire character as well as our mental health is in jeopardy if the habits of thinking are not in line with truth. Habitual thoughts determine our character.

We may develop a reputation for doing good works but not develop the character of goodness that goes with it, because our "good works" were done to be seen. It is our thought-life, our desire to do loving acts for God's sake, that develops character out of good works. Paul the apostle says in Romans 5:4 that endurance produces character; yet we all know people who have endured suffering and are wretched complainers. It is our thinking—our view of life—that makes the difference in what the circumstances of life do to us. The same circumstances can make us bitter, self-pitying abusers of life or thankful, loving saints. Our habits of thought make the difference.

In Line with the Truth

Our mental, emotional, and moral health is dependent upon how much our thoughts are in line with truth. How do we know if our thoughts are lined up with the way God made us and the universe? How do we know if our attitudes, the filters that process all input, are based on God's reality or on some distortion that will damage our characters?

Truth comes from two sources: one is God's revelation to his creatures; the other is observation of the world to discover the principles that govern humans and matter. If we accept the Scriptures as the revelation of God's purposes in this world and the principles that Almighty Wisdom has ordained for the highest good of humans, we have a plumbline to determine the truth or error of our thought patterns. The principles discovered by psychology and philosophy can be an expansion of revealed truth to the extent that they do not violate God's revealed principles. Sciences change as new "truths" are discovered. Therefore, a theory current today may be discarded tomorrow in light of further knowledge. That is why the primary plumbline is God's revelation, since the Creator knows his creation.

One of the necessary disciplines for becoming a person who can handle life's problems, according to M. Scott Peck, is dedication to the truth (*The Road Less Traveled,* pp. 44-46). First, one must acknowledge reality; second, one must respond to any new truth by incorporating it into one's thought processes and behavior.

"Almost every student entering the university believes, or says he believes, that truth is relative," according to Allan Bloom in *The Closing of the American Mind.* Intolerance is the unforgivable sin in our society, and we have been taught to fear anything absolute, not because it may be in error but because of the danger of intolerance. "Relativism is necessary to openness; and this is the virtue, the only virtue, which all primary education for more than fifty years has dedicated itself to inculcating" ([New York: Simon & Schuster, 1987], pp. 25-26).

Since we all have been affected by relativism, we find ourselves saying, "If he believes it, it's okay for him." We assume that our beliefs are private and that one belief is as valid as another. Even Christians fear intolerance and therefore are wary of those who state truths as absolutes—even statements of Jesus, such as "I am the way, and the truth, and the life; no one comes to the Father, but by me" (John 14:6). Such a statement makes seeking God through Jesus true and seeking God through Mohammed, Buddha, a guiding spirit, a guru, or by any other means false. Such statements are an embarrassment in our society.

We know it is difficult to be truly dedicated to the truth. We need to guard our statements to ourselves as well as to others. Are we stating what we know to be true, or are we hedging on the truth? The truth is not relative, and God's revelation is the ultimate source of truth. This does not mean that we must be intolerant of people who believe differently, but we, who know Jesus Christ who is Truth, must be intolerant of accepting a lie or anything false as the truth.

Exercise 31: Dedicated to Truth

1. How comfortable is it for you to say, "Jesus is the only way to the Father"?
2. In what ways is relativism compromising your integrity?
3. Imagine telling someone that what they believe is false. If this is uncomfortable, work at the wording until you are faithful to the truth and loving in your communication of it.

Sample Affirmations:

I state the truth in love.
I examine information for truth.
I seek the truth about God in the Bible

Acknowledging What Is

Another way in which we compromise the truth is to interpret events according to our filters before acknowledging the facts. A person may summarize an encounter by saying, "She doesn't like me." The incident that this person recalled by those words was actually like this: The woman walked by her with a hurried greeting. To acknowledge *what is,* rather than to leap to an emotionally weighted conclusion, would be to say, "She walked by me with only a greeting. Perhaps she was in a hurry. Perhaps she was lost in her own concerns. Perhaps she was upset by what I said to her yesterday. Or perhaps none of my interpretations are accurate. I will ask her later, and seek reality."

Self-centered people interpret the behavior of other people in terms of themselves only. "He's cross; what did I do wrong?" "She's smiling; she must be in love with me." Reality causes us to realize that we are not the sole cause of anyone else's behavior.

We are not in line with truth when we judge another person's motives. We are not mind readers and are in danger of accepting false-

Habits of Thinking

hoods when we read between the lines. Taking one "throw-away" or emotional statement of a person and making that his or her whole character or motivation usually takes us away from being in line with truth. In addition, such assumptions weigh on the negative side of our self-esteem. Passing on interpretations of the behavior of others, which is gossip, puts us in the camp of the Enemy. We are not abiding in the One Who Is the Truth.

Exercise 32: PRACTICING WHAT IS

1. Check your statements to yourself. Are you in the habit of interpreting others' behavior rather than acknowledging what is?
2. Practice acknowledging reality by stating several events that happened today in terms of *what is* rather than your interpretation of the event.
3. Review the judgments of other people you have heard recently and your response. Are you accepting biases rather than trying to state *what is?* What will you say? Gossips hate truth and those who speak it. Are you willing to lose friends to be dedicated to the truth?

Sample Affirmations:
   I state what is.
   I practice looking for reality.

Numbing Our Minds

When our minds become addicted to certain thought patterns or occupied with meaningless things, we have become effectively numb, not aware, not alert, not using our minds to God's glory.

Anything that fills our minds with untruths makes us less in tune with reality. The computer term "GIGO," garbage in–garbage out, applies to the brain as well. Whatever we put into the brain will come out in behavior. Because the human brain has a filter that interprets data, what comes out is not exactly what goes in, as with the computer. But we still reflect what we choose to absorb and what we spend our time thinking about. Absorbing and dwelling on pornography will warp the view of sex in thought, and eventually the behavior can also become warped.

Our problem with a constant diet of pulp romances is a tendency toward an emotional view of male/female relationships that is out of line with reality. A problem with a continual viewing of game shows is the tendency to develop the victim's view of life as being run by the fortune wheel. An effect of an addictive need for sports viewing is the substitution of human battles for the real battle of the kingdoms of God and Satan. The problem with horoscopes, guiding spirits, or the occult is seeking guidance from a source other than God himself through his given means of the Holy Spirit. A problem with continual talk about the affairs of people, even if we are careful not to damage anyone's reputation, is wallowing in the status quo rather than using our energy to advance God's kingdom.

Whatever we use to deaden our minds, including, of course, substance abuse, keeps us from having our minds renewed in the knowledge of God. Our minds do need rest, and many mind activities, including some of those mentioned in the paragraph above, may be restful in small doses. But many times a change of mental activity that involves a mental challenge is a mind rest that improves the mind.

Exercising the Brain

Unless we put forth effort, our minds will continue in the same thought patterns that already exist in our brains. People who do not exercise their brains are candidates for senility. Without thinking new thoughts, having fresh input, or interacting with ideas either through listening or reading, our minds atrophy.

We don't even remember the news we watch unless we interact with it in some way. The first level of thinking is simply to repeat to someone else what you have heard; this affirms the information in the mind. The next level is to interpret the information, give some meaning to it beyond just words. Next is to apply the news to one's life. The first three levels of thinking, according to Bloom's taxonomy, are knowledge, interpretation, and application. The higher levels of thinking, analysis, synthesis, and evaluation require more effort, but we can establish the habit of asking ourselves questions that stimulate the brain to these activities (Benjamin Bloom, *Taxonomy of Educational Objectives Handbook* [White Plains, N.Y.: Longman, 1977]).

To improve thinking habits, one can establish some of the following practices:

1. *Predicting:* how the story will end, what a friend will buy, or where the stock market will go. This establishes the habit of forward-thinking.

2. *Learning:* a foreign language, a subject at night school, the use of the Interlinear Bible, a musical instrument, or a new program on the computer. This brings more information into the brain to be synthesized into a greater understanding of God's world, and therefore of God himself.

3. *Visualizing:* a task before you begin it to rehearse the correct methods, a social event beforehand in order to be prepared to make the best of the relationships, or all you know about heaven (or any subject) to appreciate God more fully and to stimulate interest in researching for more information.

4. *Accepting mental challenges:* vocabulary tests (your thinking is limited by your vocabulary), crossword puzzles, mental games, remembering specific information once learned, or memorizing Scripture and poems. Using the brain becomes more fun as you exercise it more and

Habits of Thinking

puts you in the attitude of growth rather than atrophy.

5. *Discussing:* the news, movies, television shows, books, sermons, ideas, attitudes, happenings, or anything that gets beyond reporting feelings or what is. Discussing opinions, challenging ideas, and asking for feedback stimulate the brain and add a dimension to relationships. It takes more work to discuss than to report, so not all companions are willing to make the effort.

6. *Writing:* a statement, an idea, a question, an interpretation, a reaction at the end of your Bible reading, a sermon, a lecture, a movie, a television special, a book, or any other written project. Writing clarifies one's thinking. Having a notebook handy to put vague thoughts into a concrete statement exercises the brain and aids retention. There may be no need to keep these notes, since the purpose is primarily to make the information your own.

Exercise 33: MENTAL CHALLENGES

1. What mental challenges could you add to your repertoire of mental activities?
2. What mind-blanking activities do you need to abandon or limit?
3. What activities that fill your mind with false information do you want to eliminate?
4. What materials or decisions would help you establish the habit of seeking mental challenges?

Sample Affirmations:

I exercise my brain.
I look for mental challenges.

Assumptions—Lazy Habits of Thinking

Unquestioned assumptions are dangerous. Every society has certain assumptions of which its members are unaware as long as everyone around them believes the same. People often find themselves greatly offended when their assumptions—their unquestioned ways of thinking, relating, and doing—are violated. The culture shock we sometimes experience when traveling to a different country is an example of confronting people with a divergent set of assumptions. In a country where bargaining is the norm, we are wrong if we assume that giving merchants their first price gains appreciation; it only makes them regard us as fools and possibly dangerous. When we violate queues in London or wear shoes in an Indian temple, people who understand and expect adherence to such customs assume us to be crass or irreverent, although we may be simply ignorant.

Most of us assume that others think like we think. People who lie often assume that everyone lies; we tend to assume that whatever is the norm for our own lives and families is the way other people live and think as well.

When we assume that giving nations free food

Habits of Thinking

when they are hungry is helpful, we run the risk of ruining their economies. When the farmer can't sell his crop because food is free, he stops growing crops. Therefore, there is no food again next year and the next. The economies of many countries are suffering because of American assumptions.

Some time ago an organization wanting to establish a Christian service in Nepal employed local workers since locals could evangelize better than foreigners. Although the pay they gave was low compared with American standards, the organization paid almost double what local pastors were getting. Since these young men were rich by Nepali standards and not under any local authority, they were ripe for temptation. The church in Nepal suffered because of assumptions well-meaning Americans made about methods to accomplish a goal.

One of the bottom lines of American thinking is, Can we afford it? Although money is a legitimate factor in decision making, it becomes our god if it is *the* deciding factor. Money should be only one of many criteria, including what's right, what's needed, what's honest, what's helpful, what helps faith grow, and, above all, what kind of God we serve. What are his priorities? Many people of integrity in our society who place a high value on responsibility assume that to do anything that isn't fiscally sound is wrong. Yet most of us have made our greatest spiritual growth when we have felt over our heads in some dimension. If foolishness in financial matters is prompted by faith, it may be the path to spiritual growth, because God is one who likes to display his characteristics and among these are power, surprise, abundant love, and grace, all of which could be exhibited in a situation where the deciding factor was faith rather than money.

It is hard for us to know our assumptions until we run up against someone with different ones. For example, is it true that all good Christians should wear dress-up clothes to church, should use the same translation of the Bible, should agree on political and social action issues, or should avoid the same social activities? Being in other people's homes, visiting other kinds of churches, making friends with people from other cultures, and listening carefully when we see behavior that implies another value are ways to examine the assumptions that created the stereotype of the "Ugly American" and that continue to create barriers in relationships and institutions, including the church. Our assumptions need examination if we are to use our full potential.

Without compromising our faith that God is truth and that Jesus is the way, the truth, and the life, we must allow examination of important worldwide concerns so that we might be enlightened beyond our assumptions. So often Christians state positions on social issues in such a black-and-white way that other Christians are afraid to discuss the issues. Open discussion of

Habits of Thinking

differences without polarization is essential to a healthy church.

Exercise 34: BEYOND **A**SSUMPTIONS

1. List ways you can become aware of thinking habits of other cultures and ethnic groups, thus bringing to light your own assumptions.
2. How much does your church reflect the values of different economic and ethnic groups in your parish?

Sample Affirmations:

I welcome opportunities to know other cultures.
I seek to understand different viewpoints.

Habits of Anxiety

Anxiety is a continuing enemy with many manifestations. The habit of fear constricts us and must be examined and cast aside in almost all cases. All anxieties need to be examined in the light of reality. When the anxiety is specific, such as anticipation of doing a task that is new or in which one has failed in the past, we can deal with it by use of visualization. We can imagine what the worst possible outcome might be and our survival in that situation. If by examining reality we see that the outcome may be damaging to us, we can then imagine saying no and surviving the consequences of not participating. We can also counteract the fear by visualizing ourselves successfully performing the activity. Then actually trying it can begin to break the habit of that particular anxiety. Letting go of our need to avoid the activity allows our muscles to relax and can allow us to perform better.

For example, many people are afraid of public speaking, and many students are fearful of speaking in class. Those who visualize themselves answering without embarrassment and letting go of the anxiety enough to try may stumble in their answers, but each time becomes easier. At first they are anxious all class period. By letting go of the fear, they only experience the surge of adrenalin when their names are called. Next, being called on only elicits fear when they are unsure of the answer. Eventually, the cue of being called on in class doesn't arouse any fear at all whether they have an answer or not.

Another kind of specific anxiety is the need for money, which may cause us to feel like victims. Our greatest need in a situation where we feel helpless is for the creativity to come up with alternatives. A few alternatives include trade-offs, cooperative living, turning hobbies into cash, turning time into services for the elderly or working people, selling things, or even giving away encumbrances. People with restrictive habit patterns ("I can't" or "I have to") have great difficulty in situations where alternatives are

Habits of Thinking

needed. The "Yes, but" habit also limits people. Obviously, God is full of creativity and has more alternatives than we could ever imagine, so our job is to get in touch with those. Brainstorming for every possibility, no matter how impractical, is the first step in overcoming an anxiety such as the need for money. Then picturing the most likely and moving in some direction with trust that God is in control replaces anxiety with faith.

When anxiety is about the future, and we have done all we can for today, we need to realize that we can only live one day at a time. We can follow Jesus' advice that tomorrow will take care of itself. To summarize, when the anxiety is specific, several actions may help: consciously let go, imagine the worst, imagine all possible consequences, imagine alternatives, and imagine performing successfully. These mental exercises will conquer most fear. Those anxieties that are left need to be lifted up to God. We should ask for direction and wait obediently. When we have done all that God has directed, we are required to wait in faith for the Shepherd's deliverance, focusing on one day at a time. Job and Habakkuk are our models then.

A vague, unexamined fear is harder to deal with than reality. The first job is to make the anxiety specific. Keep digging until it is defined and then deal with it as with the ones above.

Anxiety manifests itself in habits that are continued long past the onset of the original fear. One evidence of unwholesome thinking habits is an automatic resistance to new suggestions. Some people automatically say no, or "Yes, but . . . " whenever a new suggestion is made. They resist change or answers, rather desiring to stay in their muddle. Their first answer is no, even if persuasion changes them later. What a joy to be around people whose automatic response is "Why not? Let's give it a try"! Eliminate the "Yes, but" syndrome.

Rigid control rather than spontaneity is another evidence of anxiety, the fear of submitting. The need to control is high in responsible people. "No one can do it as well as I. No one else will do it. Mine is the better way. I am more efficient." These and similar messages to ourselves signal the need for control. Spontaneity, the ability to go along with someone else's suggestion, is fun. Spontaneity spawns enthusiasm, and the joy of creativity and community that God intended for us is much more available with the attitude of spontaneity than with control.

Grabbing (greed) makes it difficult for people to truly give to us. Grabbing rather than waiting to receive indicates another facet of fear. The grabber is anxious about not getting his needs met or his due or his desire for pleasure fulfilled. Waiting for the mutual flow, being the giver and receiver in turn, not out of the need to control but out of the mutuality of the situation, brings release from the fear of deprivation that causes us to grab. Sometimes we grab for the biggest piece or the best position. We might cut in the line or take the best. Allowing others to give rather than grabbing, and waiting to let the situation flow by tuning into the feelings of others, are actions that can become habits that can bring freedom from the anxiety of not having enough.

Being a worrier rather than a person of great expectations represents another aspect of anxiety. The habit of worry may initially come out of concern and give evidence to the object of the worry that the worrier loves him or her. Children often ask, "Weren't you worried about me?" But when reasonable concern becomes habitual worry, a bad habit has begun. Concern causes us to be alert to our responsibility to help the loved person. Worry is lack of trust in the person and God. Worry expresses itself in nagging, in stating the unnecessary, in looking for trouble, in seeking the worst, in irritating questioning. These are not the characteristics of a person one wants to be around. This overconcern stops communication because any information will be used to undermine the confidence of the person making a decision and to impede progress with endless questions or "what if's."

The person of great expectations moves ahead confidently and is an encourager to others. God has given us victory over fear. Nothing can harm us ultimately because our eternal value and destiny are assured by the Resurrection of Jesus Christ. Therefore, we can confidently be people of great expectations.

Exercise 35: Pet Anxieties

1. What kind of anxiety are you most prone to indulge in?
2. Make an affirmation that states the intent of the new you.

Sample Affirmations:

I trust God in all matters of money.
I welcome all suggestions.
I explore alternatives in decision making.

8

Habits of Relationship

THE PATTERNS WE HAVE LEARNED TO USE IN interactions with people may be based on true or untrue information about what works in human relationships. The person who has never learned to smile will not have many smiles coming his or her way. The person who compares and criticizes will find others wary of his or her tongue. But those who listen with empathy will never lack for a companion.

Establishing habitual patterns of thinking and acting based on truths about human relationships not only eases life considerably but helps one to love, the goal of a Christian. Pulling out a good deed on special occasions or putting the best foot forward on introduction doesn't establish a continuing friendship. Characteristics that make a person a good friend, such as respect, appreciation, and kindness, contribute to good relationships only if they are *habits*.

Respect and *Agape*-love

Respect is the basic evidence of love. To love your neighbor *as yourself* implies that your neighbor has as much value as you do. The word "respect" usually indicates the valuing of another as an equal, while the word "love" often implies sexual emotion or need, and "charity" has come to be applied only to dealings with an inferior. Therefore, the word "respect" may come closest to meaning *agape*-love. Respect is shown by regarding the other person's feelings and rights as having as much validity as our own. The result of true respect or *agape*-love is to be able to weep with those who weep and rejoice with those who rejoice. We identify or empathize with all humans as though their situations were our own.

What does the habit of respect look like? Where does our *agape*-love break down?

One of the symbols of respect is waiting your turn, whether in line, in traffic, or in games. It is easy to feel that our time and our needs are far more important than those of others. But respect tells us that their tired feet, television program, or need to chat with the clerk is as important to them as our needs are to us.

Children and the elderly are often disregarded as equals. The middle part of life becomes fast-paced. To take the time to listen to a child whose conversation seems meaningless, or to a senior citizen who is slow and repetitive, seems too much to ask of a busy middle-life person. The

Habits of Relationship

habit of truly listening shows respect for people's feelings and for their need to communicate.

We're often tempted not to consider people with handicaps as equals because we fear that they might take our precious time, or that we, except for the grace of God, could be as they. Yet their feelings and needs are the same as ours. They have equal claim as our "neighbors."

The habit of seeing the needs around us is part of *agape*-love. Jesus said that whatever we do for one of "the least of these" (hungry, thirsty, homeless, poor, sick, or prisoners) we do for Christ (Matt. 25:40). Our equality becomes more apparent when we realize that God's love is for the world, for each individual in the world, and that his ministry is particularly for the poor, the disabled, and the dispossessed. When we give respect, time, and listening to any human being, but particularly to those who are powerless, we are participating in God's love. This awareness of God's love for all and willingness to respect all gives us the foundation to establish habits of love.

Exercise 36: Respect

1. What kind of people do you have the hardest time treating as equals?
2. Choose one person (or type of person) and decide one way in which you can show respect each time you encounter him or her.

Sample Affirmations:

I affirm that all humans have equal value with me.

I treat the dispossessed as God's beloved.

Thankfulness

Thanks is one expression of appreciation and respect. In Romans 1:18-23, Paul talks about the downfall of humans, and the lack of thankfulness was listed as step one. When people didn't recognize God as the Creator *and give thanks,* their minds became darkened. Our perspective on life, people, the environment, animals, plants, even material objects and mechanical devices changes when we learn the habit of thankfulness. Our relationships with all creation come to be based on a thankful attitude.

The simple habit of saying "thank you" is a great starter because it smoothes human relations. Many of us have experienced going out of our way to drive a person home or to do an errand for someone and receiving no appreciation. Lack of the other's appreciation makes us feel like a servant, disregarded as an equal who has as many things of importance to do as the asker. A "thank you" or other immediate display of appreciation makes us feel that we are regarded as equals.

Sometimes the asker or imposer intends to write a note or buy a gift or return the favor later. But an immediate response is important to keep the relationship free of resentment. Even in boss-employee or parent-child relations, a "thank you" helps the doer feel respected and not just used.

Family members are particularly guilty of using one another without evidence of appreciation. Often one member of the family is left to care for an elderly member. Even though she or he accepts the responsibility, a word of appreciation from other family members is tremendously meaningful.

Almost all family members feel that they are giving something that isn't being appreciated. Seeing the other persons' work or gifts, even if it doesn't seem nearly as great as our own, and speaking our appreciation, even if we don't feel appreciated, is an important step. Usually when the other people feel appreciated, they can begin to appreciate in turn. Even if the appreciation is not returned, we have helped fill a gap in another's life that will make him more appreciative of others. This is *agape*-love, which includes giving regardless of whether the giving is returned.

To make thankfulness a habit, we need prompts or cues. Leaving a person is a good cue to think of whatever thanks we can give. Meals, specific sights, beauty, awaking, getting into or out of a car, or any other regular happening can become a cue for giving thanks to God. When we establish the habit of giving thanks to God, it usually spills over to people, too. However, we need to consciously set both patterns.

Exercise 37: THANKFULNESS

1. What cues will you use to establish the habit of thanks to God?
2. When do you need to say thanks to people?
3. Try visualizing yourself as a thankful, appreciative person in all circumstances.

Sample Affirmations:

I am a thankful, appreciative person.
I remember to thank God and people regularly.

Appreciation

Noticing the pleasing attributes of others and communicating that awareness is the essence of appreciation. Compliments about a person's appearance are probably the most common. However, we need to notice voices, eyes, smiles, people's ways of handling situations, their concerns, their capabilities, their availability to help—all kinds of attributes that we can appreciate. Appreciation is broader than thanks.

When a person complains about others, it is often because he feels unappreciated. Although we would each hope to become mature enough not to need the notice of others to sustain our good works or a positive self-image, few of us can achieve that high ideal. Therefore, we need to act as emissaries of God to show the love that our Creator radiates to all of us.

Sometimes we feel it is insincere to compliment someone if we feel critical about other aspects of his or her life. A man may yell at his wife, be obnoxious to his kids, and drive like a kamikaze pilot, but treat his dog with kindness and wisdom. We might be tempted to ignore his one good trait, or to say, "Why don't you treat people as well as you treat your dog?" However, a sincere compliment on his good handling of the dog will be more effective in showing respect and helping him respect himself than any criticism. It is helpful to state appreciation for seemingly minor good traits when glaring major bad traits are present. The habit of looking for the good and declaring it is *agape*-love.

Teachers are trained to find and appreciate one positive behavior in a pesky child. By focusing on the good trait, a persistent teacher can often turn a child around. Adults respond equally well to appreciation.

God's command to love means to act for the best of the other person; it has nothing to do with our feelings. And when we choose to do what is right, our feelings follow. When we form our lips into a smile, the feeling of smiling gradually emerges. When we change our position from a slouch to leaning toward the speaker, we gradually change our attitude from boredom to interest. When we give a compliment to someone, we feel better about that person.

Since actions change attitude, one doesn't need to wait for a change of heart to change these attitudes. Act on the positive side and the attitude will change.

Exercise 38: COMPLIMENTS

1. Think of a time when you criticized rather than finding the good trait to appreciate.
2. What cues can you use to establish the habit of appreciation instead of criticism? Perhaps the desire to criticize can be turned into a cue for finding a trait to compliment.
3. Decide what kind of action would change the attitude you want to work on.

Sample Affirmations:

I compliment people regularly.
I look for things to appreciate in people.
I do what is loving.

Kindness and Ritual Greetings

Many of the courtesies we used to call "common courtesies" were based on kindness: saying "please" and "excuse me"; holding the door for the next person; picking up what someone has dropped; offering to help carry a heavy load, even for a stranger; offering help in time of need. All of these acts are evidence of being aware of the people around us as human beings worth caring for.

Part of respect is greeting people. If someone walks by without speaking, it makes one feel like a non-person. Those people who greet everybody when they enter a room are considered friendly people. They are approachable. Smiling, eye-contact, and being able to laugh at oneself establish a person as approachable. The silent ones, the eye-avoiders, create discomfort. Greetings are repetitions of the same somewhat meaningless words: "How are you?" "Fine, and you?" These are not meant to be conversation; they are ritual and serve the role of greasing the wheels of social life. Rituals are an important part of comfort.

Exercise 39: AWARENESS

1. What evidences of kindness have you become careless about or never developed?

Sample Affirmation:

I am aware of and kind to all people around me.

Conversational Habits

Since conversation is one of the basic tools of relating to others, our habits of conversing, speaking, and listening have a strong role in how well we relate. If our voices are not clear and pleasant, people may find it hard to listen to us. Mumbling, repeating unnecessary words or sounds, looking away, throat clearing, or speaking that is raspy, high pitched, piercing, or irritating are all bad habits that can usually be changed. Since we don't notice these things ourselves, we need to ask a friend to make us aware.

An equal or more important part of speaking is what we say. We all have habitual subject matter that we introduce into conversations. Details about one's health and family life are generally boring or embarrassing to people who are not intimate friends. Constant or vicious criticism of others is usually uncomfortable for the listeners. Negative outlooks are downers. People enjoy humor, a happy spirit, well-told stories of things that have happened, discussions of current events, movies, television programs, and sometimes job- or interest-related subjects. Although listening is a far more important skill than speaking, we can still be aware of how we sound and what we contribute.

Exercise 40: Conversational Habits

1. How do you sound? Ask someone to honestly tell you or listen to a tape of yourself. What bad habits do you want to change? Awareness may be sufficient to make desired habit changes of this kind.

2. What are your topics of conversation? Do you bore or embarrass people with too much detail or too much self-centered talk? Do you have enough information of general interest to carry on a conversation that would interest someone?
3. Do you need practice in telling an incident in a way that entertains? Tape yourself, critique, revise, then tape again and listen.

Sample Affirmations:

I converse on many topics.
I tell a story well.

Habits of Listening

Listening is the gift we all want from another person because it means someone is interested in us. We can all form the habit of disciplining our minds to truly listen. The good listener looks at the speaker, gives his or her mind totally to understanding what the speaker is saying, asks questions to clarify, nods or murmurs occasionally to indicate assent, and gives statements that assure the speaker that he or she is understood. We listen with our eyes, our face, our minds, our affirmations, and our questions.

Most people listen with half of their minds on what they are going to say or on their own thoughts, either indicating boredom by their lack of attention or pretending to listen with appropriate nods and murmurs but providing no depth of response. Listening is hard work and one of the highest evidences of love. The non-listener is self-centered, choosing shallowness rather than love.

The purpose of questions in conversation is to give the other person a chance to express what he wants to. Questions that are impersonal (What do you think of the weather?) keep conversation very superficial and make it boring after three minutes. Questions that are very personal (Why did your husband leave you?) can make a person feel uncomfortable and want to avoid being around that conversationalist. (It would make a much more interesting conversation, however!) A conversationalist is expected to earn the right to ask a truly personal question.

The hardest part of a conversation is finding a common topic to discuss or a hook-in question to get the other person going. We generally ask about work, studies, travel, hometown, or a current event to get started. A person can offer a short incident that is current: "On my way over here I saw . . . "; "Yesterday at work I experienced . . . "

Interesting conversations between strangers or friends can develop from the lead-in question, "What do you think about . . . ?" A person's thought responses are usually not as personal as his or her feeling responses. At least the question is more impersonal. Asking questions helps us

Habits of Relationship

learn. Ros Rinker, a gifted personal evangelist, used to say that everybody is an expert on something. If you are interested in learning, there is something you can learn from everyone. And of course, we all love being the "expert." A good lead-in is "What are your hobbies?" But we must *listen* to the answers.

Deep friendship is based on shared feelings; asking questions to allow feelings to be shared is a friendship skill. "How do you feel about . . ." is a lead-in phrase that can become part of one's conversational habit pattern. The topic of the question can be anything that is of interest to both conversationalists: How do you feel about the holiday season? The sermon? Your dog? Putting your mother in a rest home? Getting a promotion? Each of these subjects evokes feeling. The opportunity to express that feeling clarifies it for those sharing and helps them to grow as human beings. Therefore, asking questions about a person's feelings is an important pattern to establish. Of course, to ask the question and not listen, or not wait for the answer, is admitting your lack of interest in the other person. They catch on fast.

Exercise 41: THE HABIT OF LISTENING

1. How do you rank yourself in drawing out others?
2. What listening skills do you need to improve on: eye-contact, waiting, facial

response, appropriate confirming statements?
3. What kinds of questioning skills do you want to establish as part of your conversational habits?

Sample Affirmations:

I listen with my mind and my face.
I help people express themselves by asking appropriate questions.
I am interested in knowing people.

Habits of Generosity

The habit of generosity is another indication of *agape*-love. A tight, grasping, poverty-oriented attitude gives evidence of an inner poverty of the heart. Those of us who grew up with Depression-minded parents may have to fight against the attitude of saving every penny. Our heavenly Father owns the world and has promised to take care of us.

God is full of delightful serendipities, the unexpected gift of joy. We can learn to be spontaneous givers of delight. We can afford to be as generous with others as we are with ourselves, or better yet, as God is with us. To be socially correct, we must send cards to those who sent to us and invite those who invited us. This is fine but not enough, according to Jesus. He tells us to give to those who cannot return the gift—not to make *ourselves* feel good, not giving a gift *we* choose for them, but finding what *they* want or need and giving for *their* joy.

Relational Hazards

The lists of sins in the Bible are full of emotional habits that damage us—jealousy, hatred, strife, deceit, gossip, slander, haughtiness, boasting, faithlessness, heartlessness, envy. Most of these hurtful, defensive habits of thought and action began when we were young and uncertain of being loved. These habits serve no purpose for us, as adults who have accepted God's overwhelming love for us.

If we totally eliminate the habit of comparing ourselves with others and luxuriate in the love and purposes God has for us, we will greatly diminish the likelihood of giving in to any of these ugly temptations. The attitude of generosity resting on the foundation of God's total and eternal love for us and others is a good counteraction to the distress of relational sins.

Exercise 42: Emotional Habits

1. Which of your emotional habits are most damaging to you?
2. Receive God's picture of you, love for you, and forgiveness, in place of your

need to defend yourself or put yourself down.

Sample Affirmations:

   I give a little extra.
   I am generous.
   I give because God gives.

9

Balancing Habits

SINCE ESTABLISHING A NEW HABIT TAKES energy and at least three or four weeks of time, and since we can only work on one or two habits at a time, choosing where to put our energy is important.

We are physical creatures who need good habits to maintain our bodies and environment. We are spiritual beings who long to pursue our union with God. We are thinking souls who need to seek truth, and we are relational/emotional people who need to love and be loved. In all of these areas we have good habits and bad habits.

Since our society overemphasizes the physical and material aspects of life, we need to tackle our physical habits with the godly motivations of achieving good health and a healthy environment in order to accomplish our life goals.

Change Your Bad Habits for Good!

Physical Habits

"Physical training is of some value, but godliness has value for all things, holding promise for both the present life and the life to come" (I Tim. 4:8 NIV). Spiritual, mental, and relational habits have far more value than physical habits, but life is easier and better if we also have our bodies and environments under control.

Fitness begins with exercise. Three kinds of exercise need to be part of our daily routine in order for us to maintain good health: exercises for flexibility, for strength, and for endurance.

Flexibility is primarily maintained by stretching. A cat serves as a wonderful model of stretching and flexibility. Stretches can be done in a daily set or they can be hooked into other routines.

By following a television exercise program or an exercise tape, a person can decide which stretches are needed daily. Our bodies will tell us which are not part of our daily routines.

If we choose to hook the stretches into our daily routine rather than do them all at once, we need to choose where each one will fit. We could do a full body stretch before getting out of bed, a leg stretch while drying the legs after showering, a neck stretch to check the driveway before backing out, a shoulder stretch by leaning through a doorway while the shower water is warming up, a body twist while waiting in line at the super-

Balancing Habits

market, and arm swings at the beginning of a walk.

Exercise 43: Flexibility

1. What stretches do you need?
2. Where will you fit them into a daily routine?

Sample Affirmation:

I stretch my entire body regularly.

Strength is maintained by tensing the muscles that need strengthening. Depending upon our sex and age, we may choose to maintain strength in different parts of our bodies. However, certain muscles always need maintenance in order for us to be in good health.

Many older people have difficulties with balance and getting out of chairs. Balance can be maintained by standing to put on one's pants every day. If we start wobbling we can practice, just as we did when we were children. Leg muscles can be maintained by lifting an old bag filled with cans of food while watching television.

Abdominal muscles keep our organs in place and must be exercised by regularly tensing them in order to maintain health. By looking at your body in the mirror, you can see neck, back, or shoulder muscles that are not holding the body frame in place. These need to be strengthened.

Tension, or tightening of the muscles, can be attained through exercises such as sit-ups or push-ups, or by tensing the muscles and holding that pressure for ten seconds or longer, depending upon the degree of strength one is attempting to achieve.

Exercise 44: STRENGTH

1. Choose the muscles you want to exercise.
2. Choose the cues and time and method to accomplish this.

Sample Affirmation:

My body is strong.

Endurance is also essential for health. Although the exercises for flexibility and strength can be fit into daily schedules without taking much extra time, sedentary people will find that maintaining endurance for good metabolism, a healthy heart and lungs, and general well-being does require sustained effort, at the very least twenty minutes three times per week.

A few people maintain sports on a regular basis throughout their lives, and some people continue to work at activities that raise the heartbeat, but most of us need to establish the habit of walking, one of the most effective exercises for endurance.

Since habits are automatic responses, the idea of doing something three times a week is hard to make automatic. To establish the habit of

Balancing Habits

walking, it needs to consistently follow the same cue. Walking with a friend can be fun, and many people feel safer and more committed to the habit if a friend is counting on them for a joint walk. Walking is so essential to health that it needs to be as much a part of the weekly schedule as work.

If walking or any endurance exercise is not part of your life, begin with a little step, a walk around the block. Build up gradually as your body adjusts to the new comfort zone.

Exercise 45: Endurance
1. What endurance exercise are you scheduling? Do you need more information for motivation or knowledge? Do you need proper shoes or clothing?
2. What cue will signal your exercise? Plan the time and place and partners.

Sample Affirmation:

My body is fit.

Eating Habits

The American concept of dieting seems to have been removed from health. Our eating habits are often dictated either by vanity or by emotional needs rather than by the correct purpose—good health.

Good eating habits begin with memorizing the

basic food groups. The four currently used are cereals and grains, meat and fish, milk and dairy products, and fruit and vegetables. The number of portions of each needed daily varies slightly by age and activity, but we need two to four portions of each daily, chosen from a variety of foods, to gain the nutrition to keep us healthy.

The long-term goal is to automatically eat what our bodies need and to eliminate those items that are detrimental. However, knowing that our comfort zones change slowly, a wise person chooses to make one change at a time—cutting down on fat by eliminating certain deep-fried foods, for example. After four to six weeks, when one change is automatic, we can tackle another. Plan the changes one at a time, and after a year the effects will be healthier and longer lasting than those of any crash diet. Continued reading about good nutrition will help motivate us and give us the best information as we choose our next steps.

Exercise 46: EATING

1. What information do you need about nutrition, and where are you going to get it?
2. What one habit do you want to change to better eating habits?

Sample Affirmations:

I eat only what I need.
I eat only what my body needs.

Balancing Habits

Organizational Habits

Most Americans accumulate too many possessions. We can focus more clearly on the important elements of life—loving God, loving people, and taking our role in God's battle against evil—if our time is not consumed by care of possessions. If every possession has its own place and we establish the habit of putting it in its place, much of the possession-battle is won. If maintenance is habitual, so that it requires little decision making or upset, another battle is won.

Possessions—things—can be organized; people can't. Time management often puts people and things in the same category, giving the impression that people can be managed. Relationships of love are fluid, and all of our contacts with people belong in the love category.

EXERCISE 47: POSSESSIONS / TIME

1. What possessions do you need to get rid of or find a place for?
2. How can some of your maintenance time be freed for higher priorities related to your life goals?

CONCLUSION

It is easy to use the power of habits to serve personal gain rather than to become the persons God intended us to be. We need to become conscious of the cultural biases that influence our priorities, then—by examining God's priorities—bring our own habits in line with truth and reality. We also will be blessed by recognizing the rhythm of time and the seasons of life in developing habits that will serve us well for a lifetime.

Perhaps you have tried some of the exercises. Perhaps you have kept a record of your thoughts. Now is the time to find your own balance and begin to make the changes you desire. Remember! The comfort zone can be stretched only a little bit at a time, so you will be working on changes the rest of your life. But that's what life is all about. God bless!